This is Timothy Paul Jc
Always wrestling with the hardest of p
holding out the faith once for all delivered to the saints. This
is an essential resource for contemplating and critiquing
contemporary attacks on the trustworthiness of the Bible.

Dan DeWitt
Associate Professor of Apologetics, Cedarville University,
Cedarville, Ohio
author of *Life in the Wild*

Why Should I Trust the Bible? steps inside our most
challenging doubts about the Bible and shows us a way
out to faith in its truthfulness. Written in an disarmingly
honest and straightforward way, Timothy Paul Jones' down-
to-earth stories and up-to-date scholarship create a space in
our skeptical world for authentic belief in the Bible. Highly
recommended!

Mark D. Allen
Executive Director, Center for Apologetics and Cultural
Engagement at Liberty University, Lynchburg, Virginia
coauthor of *Apologetics at the Cross*

With humility, wit, and compelling research, Timothy Paul
Jones masterfully answers the question: 'Why would any
reasonable person in the twenty-first-century trust that the
Bible is true?' Read this book to find out how someone who

once struggled to trust the Bible now believes this book and defends its truth.

Jamaal Williams
lead pastor, Sojourn Church Midtown, Louisville, Kentucky

Timothy Paul Jones humbly asks, 'Why would any reasonable person in the twenty-first century trust that the Bible is true?' This is a courageous question for an evangelical theologian to admit in an age of scepticism! It's the question that many image bearers contemplate inside and outside the church, and we should not fear these questioners. We must converse with them in ways that embody grace and truth. This faithful resource will strengthen your ability to do so.

Curtis A. Woods
associate executive director for the Kentucky Baptist Convention;
assistant professor of applied theology, The Southern Baptist
Theological Seminary, Louisville, Kentucky

The Bible has been subject to attack like no other book in history. Timothy Paul Jones has provided an excellent resource that draws together some of the most reliable, contemporary scholarship in order to demonstrate why the Bible remains a trustworthy book. With particular emphasis on the Gospels he shows that regardless of debates over the details there is no reason to deny the essential, historical value of the New Testament writings. Findings from scholarship are often misused against faith in Christ, this book puts the record straight.

Chris Sinkinson
Lecturer in Old Testament and Apologetics
Moorlands College, Sopley, Christchurch, Dorset

THE BIG TEN
Critical Questions Answered

SERIES EDITORS
James N. Anderson and Greg Welty

Why Should I Trust the Bible?

Timothy Paul **Jones**

CHRISTIAN
FOCUS

Copyright © Timothy Paul Jones 2019

paperback ISBN 978-1-5271-0474-7
epub ISBN 978-1-5271-0514-0
mobi ISBN 978-1-5271-0515-7

Published in 2019
by
Christian Focus Publications Ltd,
Geanies House, Fearn, Ross-shire
IV20 1TW, Scotland
www.christianfocus.com

Cover design by Paul Lewis

Printed and bound by
Bell & Bain, Glasgow

CONTENTS

For Skylar Raylynn

This book was forged in the pain
of walking with you through
the hardest months of your life.

I knew that 'our God … is able to deliver'—
But the shadow was always so dark and so near:
'But if not.'

And then one day,
the light began to dawn,
and the girl I once knew
came back.
And I loved her more
than ever before.

1

A Difficult Book to Believe?

The Bible is a difficult book to believe.

If you try to read the Bible from the beginning, you'll find yourself face to face with a talking snake and enchanted fruit before you've finished the first three chapters. When you run across such plot devices in the works of Rudyard Kipling or the brothers Grimm, you immediately recognize them as surefire marks of a fable or a fairy tale. In the Bible, they somehow qualify as history. Before you reach the final page of the first book of the Bible, the Almighty has already drowned most of humanity and obliterated entire cities with fire from the sky. In the second book of the saga, God calls for a conquest that sets the stage for more than a millennium of multinational bloodletting over a scrap of land smaller than the entirety of Great Britain. After all this, the virgin birth and resurrection that show up in the opening books of the New Testament actually seem somewhat tame. At the same time, divine conception seems like it could be an all-too-convenient strategy to explain an unplanned pregnancy, and it doesn't take many trips to the graveyard before you realize resurrection is far from the most common outcome for a corpse.

Atheist biologist Richard Dawkins has defined the Bible as 'a chaotically cobbled-together anthology of disjointed documents, composed, revised, translated, distorted and "improved" by hundreds of anonymous authors, editors, and copyists, unknown to us and mostly unknown to each other, spanning nine centuries.'[1] I would quibble with certain portions of Dawkins's description, but he's not entirely wrong when it comes to the processes that brought the good book from the Ancient Near East to us. 'I have come to regard with some suspicion those who claim the Bible never troubles them,' Rachel Held Evans mused after a year of attempting to follow the teachings of Scripture with comedic and quasi-literalistic scrupulosity. 'I can only assume this means they haven't actually read it.'[2]

Why, then, would anyone believe that the Bible is true?

---

1   Richard Dawkins, *The God Delusion* (New York: Mariner, 2008), 268.

2   Rachel Held Evans, *A Year of Biblical Womanhood* (Nashville: Thomas Nelson, 2012), 51.

Rachel Held Evans's observation provides a partial explanation. There *are* millions of people who trust the Bible without ever reading it or reflecting on its strangeness. And yet, that's far from the whole story. There are also millions of people around the world and throughout history who have wrestled deeply with what the Bible has to say, and yet they've still somehow ended up believing it. And that brings us to the dilemma that I plan to explore throughout this book: Why would any reasonable person in the twenty-first century trust that the Bible is true?

WHO SHOULD—AND SHOULDN'T—READ THIS BOOK ABOUT THE BIBLE?

It is possible that you're someone who's perfectly willing to believe a story with or without evidence. Perhaps you re-post stories on social media without ever checking to see if they might be urban legends. Maybe it's never occurred to you that believing a sacred text that exalts a wandering miracle-worker who's been missing from this planet for almost two thousand years is at least slightly strange. If that's you, don't bother reading this book, because I didn't write this book with you in mind.

This book is aimed at a very different sort of individual.

The words that I've penned in these pages are for people who fact-check every claim they see on social media and second-guess almost every story they hear. When it comes to trusting the Bible, this book is for people for whom skepticism has at some point felt more natural than faith.

In short, it's for people who are a lot like me.

I haven't always been this way. Truth be told, I spent nearly two decades of my life assuming that conversations with an invisible friend were perfectly normal, as long as that friend's name happened to be Jesus. I didn't always do what I was told that Jesus desired. And yet, I never doubted that he was present, watching me from a gilded throne somewhere along the hemline of the Milky Way.

Those assumptions began to fall apart for me at a library desk in a college town on the plains of north-east Kansas. For me, that desk became an altar where one form of faith died three decades ago and a better set of beliefs rose to take its place.

Lies I learned about the Bible

I started college in the gap between U2's *Rattle and Hum* and *Achtung Baby!* albums, in the year that Macauley Culkin stayed home alone and Wilson Phillips held on for one more day. Prior to my first semester of college, it had never occurred to me to question anything I read in the Bible. In the churches that my family attended, any doubts about the Bible were met with a curious combination of hubris and fear. The polyester-clad pastors of these churches seemed cocksure that there were no problems or difficulties to be found in the Scriptures. And yet, even the slightest question about potential difficulties seemed to trigger terrified outbursts at the decadent culture in which our church stood as a lonely fortress of authentic faith. Every word of the King James Version of the Bible had to be taken literally, every line of separation drawn sharply, every ideological barrier built high.

In my early teenage years, the proofs that I heard bellowed from those plywood pulpits seemed ironclad. I knew the earth had to be thousands of years old—not billions—because one pastor had shown us a photograph of human and dinosaur footprints fossilized side-by-side in the Paluxy riverbed in Texas. I trusted the hand-copied manuscripts that preceded our printed Bibles because a speaker at a preaching conference had told us that these words had been preserved for thousands of years without a single copying variation, if you looked in the right manuscripts. I knew the Bible had to be precise even in the most minute scientific details because I'd heard about astronomers at NASA who found a mysterious gap in planetary movements from the distant past; the missing time remained a mystery until the scientists corrected their calculations to include the time when the sun 'hasted not to go down about a whole day' according to the book of Joshua in the Bible (Joshua 10:13, KJV). As far as I could tell, the only reason that anyone might find it difficult to trust the Bible was because they were rejecting evidences that were obvious to everyone.

And then I went to college.

No one in my family had ever earned a college degree, so I had no idea what to expect when I started classes that August. It was a Christian college, and most of the professors believed the Bible—but not in the same way that I'd been taught to believe the Bible. When I mentioned the Paluxy riverbed footprints in a class discussion of the book of Genesis, the professor seemed unimpressed and asked for citations that referenced newspapers or academic journals. It wasn't long before I discovered that the evidences I had heard from the lips of preachers and conference speakers were little more than fundamentalist urban legends. NASA has never misplaced a day; not one of the surviving hand-copied portions of the New Testament agrees completely with all the others; and the fossilized footprints in Texas were never human in the first place. There were other similar claims that had shaped my childhood theology as well. And yet, the more I learned, the more these meager evidences began to fracture under an uncomfortable freight of facts.

It was around this time that I began working evening shifts at a library to pay my way through college. Each evening, after shelving the books that had been returned that day, it was my responsibility to monitor a mostly empty library from a desk near the entrance—which provided me with access to tens of thousands of books and plenty of time. What I discovered while re-shelving books and magazines was a deep ore of writings that resonated with my growing frustration with the fabricated claims that had supported my faith. One of the first such books I read was Bertrand Russell's bluntly-labeled collection of essays *Why I Am Not a Christian.* After that, I found a book by G. A. Wells that asked *Did Jesus Exist?,* followed by a mixed bag of conspiracy theories about the resurrection of Jesus. Not all of the books were equally convincing, but every one of them chipped away at assumptions I had held since childhood.

Summer faded into fall, the leaves of the trees along the Kaw River turned gold then brown and tumbled to the ground, and night after night I kept seeking out more books that challenged my faith. By the time winter leached the last remnants of green from the patchwork of wheat fields that surrounded this college town, I was skimming early papers from the Jesus Seminar and consuming as many back issues of *The Humanist* magazine as I could find. I plowed through every book on the stack of shelves labeled 'Atheism', and I was enthralled. Each text felt like an intellectual feast of forbidden fruit, thrilling yet chilling because I was gingerly treading pathways that I had never even considered before. At some point in that journey, I passed through a door that I did not recognize until it was behind me. When I turned to look back through the door, I saw the faith I had learned in the churches of my adolescent years crumbling into ashes on the other side. I do not miss it.

THE LAST PARTICLES OF FAITH

In the opening pages of his novel *In the Beauty of the Lilies*, John Updike traced the collapse of a fictional pastor's faith: 'Down in the parsonage of the Fourth Presbyterian Church,' Updike wrote:

> the Reverend Clarence Arthur Wilmot ... felt the last particles of his faith leave him. The sensation was distinct—a visceral surrender, a set of dark sparkling bubbles escaping upward. ... Clarence's mind was like a many-legged wingless insect that had long and tediously been struggling to climb up the walls of a slick-walled porcelain basin; and now a sudden impatient wash of water swept it down into the drain. There is no God.[3]

I first read Updike's words nearly a decade after that year at the library desk, but I still recalled the sensation that this novelist so vividly described. I had felt the desperate scramble to find some small foothold of faith amid a flood of alternate possibilities, followed by an impatient wash of water that swept the last fragments of faith away.

The more I read, the more it seemed that Jesus—the deity I'd been taught to trust without question, a crucified

---

3   John Updike, *In the Beauty of the Lilies* (New York: Random House, 1996), 4-6.

God-man raised from the dead and someday returning to earth again—might be as mythical as NASA's missing day. For the first time in my life, I sensed the strangeness of supposing that the Bible was true and that a once-deceased man had exited a tomb two thousand years ago. I found myself considering carefully whether any of the stories in the Bible could be trusted. What if the real Jesus of Nazareth, who meandered back and forth between first-century Judea and Galilee, was quite different from the Jesus described in the Bible? Or what if Jesus never existed at all? These questions and dozens of others like them were the queries that set me on the path that has shaped every aspect of my life since those months in the library. A doctoral dissertation on the psychology of faith, graduate and undergraduate courses in biblical languages and ancient history, research into how stories pass from one generation to the next in oral cultures, time spent with a storyteller in the Lakota tribe of Native Americans to learn about stabilizing factors in oral traditions—all of it can be traced back to the questions that no one had prepared me to answer during those nights beneath the fluorescent lights that hung between the stacks of books in the library.

SURPRISED BY JOY

I lived as a hypocrite during those months of exploring other perspectives. Week by week, I played piano in the tiny church where my father preached, my fingers forming all the right chords even as I doubted every clause I saw suspended between the bass and treble clefs. Most Sundays, I left church believing less than I had when I arrived. I had pressed against every evidence for faith that I had been provided, and the entire structure had collapsed almost without resistance.

'Don't believe in forced entry, don't believe in rape/but every time she passes by wild thoughts escape/... Don't believe in excess, success is to give/don't believe in riches but you should see where I live,' was how U2 described their inconsistencies on *Rattle and Hum*.[4] Repeated on a cassette player in the salvaged station wagon that I drove back and forth to college, Bono's hymn to his hypocrisies became the soundtrack for my own. I played the songs and I played the part, but the faith I once knew was gone.

And yet, oddly enough, this growing sense of skepticism was no more satisfying than the faith I had left behind. The faithlessness I felt at this point and the anemic faith I had known before both offered a different stack of claims, laid out in lifeless piles like organs on an autopsy table. The stack on the side of skepticism looked more substantive at the moment. And yet, both options seemed denuded of beauty and wonder. Each possibility offered a conglomeration of

---

4   U2, 'God Part II', *Rattle and Hum* (Island, 1988).

differently-configured claims, but neither one offered a satisfying story.

It was an Irishman whose name I previously knew only from novels who cracked open the window of my mind to a new set of possibilities. Some of C.S. Lewis's fictional works had been banned in one of the Christian schools I had attended as a teenager (to this day, I'm still not certain why). As a result, I was intrigued when I learned that this novelist—some of whose works had apparently been too risqué for blossoming fundamentalists—had produced dozens of books and essays defending the coherence of Christian faith.

The text from C.S. Lewis that captivated me most deeply wasn't *Mere Christianity*, his most explicit case for Christian faith. Still today, *Mere Christianity* seems to me to intertwine some of Lewis's best analogies with his weakest arguments. It was *Surprised by Joy*—a meandering spiritual autobiography that traced the author's journey from atheism to theism and finally to Christianity—that had the greatest impact on my thinking as a college student.

What I recognized as I read *Surprised by Joy* was that a rejection of faith wasn't the only possible response to the deluge of difficulties I was now glimpsing for the first time. What's more, certain questions that seemed new and shocking to me—the possibility that the Gospels might be mythologized echoes of pagan stories, for example, or that the Gospels might not be historical at all—weren't really new. Long before my first tentative journey through the pages of Bertrand Russell's *Why I Am Not a Christian*, others had wrestled with these same difficulties and landed in a very different place when it came to the plausibility of faith. This became particularly apparent to me when Lewis described how he, as a professor of literature, had once struggled to accept the testimony of the New Testament Gospels. 'I was too experienced in literary criticism,' he wrote,

> to regard the Gospels as myths. They had not the mythical taste. And yet the very matter which they set down in their artless, historical fashion ... was precisely the matter of great myths. If ever a myth had become a fact, had been incarnated, it would be just like this. And nothing else in all literature was just like this. Myths were like it in one way. Histories were like it in another, but nothing was simply alike. And no person was like the Person it depicted.[5]

It wasn't merely Lewis's intellectual arguments that captured my attention, though. It was how he responded to difficult questions by weaving together words that lived and breathed and laughed and made sense of human nature and history. When considering pagan parallels to the stories of Jesus in *Surprised by Joy* and *God in the Dock*, Lewis didn't deny the

---

5   C.S. Lewis, *Surprised by Joy* (New York: Harcourt Brace, 1955), 228.

similarities. Instead, he opened the door to a new way of seeing the parallels:

> The old myth of the Dying God, without ceasing to be myth, comes down from the heaven of legend and imagination to the earth of history. It happens—at a particular date, in a particular place, followed by definable historical consequences. We pass from a Balder or an Osiris, dying nobody knows when or where, to a historical Person crucified ... under Pontius Pilate. ... We must not be nervous about 'parallels' and 'Pagan Christs': they ought to be there—it would be a stumbling block if they weren't.[6]

When I read Lewis's *The Problem of Pain,* I also encountered for the first time in my life a believer in Jesus who openly embraced what seemed a rather obvious fact to me by this point, that the cosmos as we know it has developed and grown more complex over billions of years.[7] The awareness that it was conceivable to follow Jesus without denying the deep antiquity of the cosmos removed a massive stumbling block for me. I work with many Christians who believe the earth was formed only a few thousand years ago, and I respect their perspectives. And yet, I find myself still today in a very different place on this issue than some of my colleagues, believing that an earth that was born billions of

---

6   C.S. Lewis, *God in the Dock* (Grand Rapids: Eerdmans, 1970), 58-60.

7   C.S. Lewis, *The Problem of Pain* (New York: Harper, 1940), 2-3.

years ago is the only way to make comprehensive sense of the geological and astronomical evidence.

While reading the works of Lewis, I also ran across a book entitled *The New Testament Documents: Are They Reliable?* by F.F. Bruce. Bruce's writing lacked Lewis's eloquence and wit, but I found in these chapters a similar openness to engaging real problems and difficulties on the basis of evidence. I began consuming not only books that rejected Christianity but also the works of believers who were wrestling with the biblical text from a multiplicity of perspectives. I read everything I could find by C.S. Lewis and F.F. Bruce, all the while still reading atheistic texts like Carl Sagan's *Cosmos* and an introduction to the Bible penned by Isaac Asimov.

Not all the books I read were equally convincing. Yet, as I studied each one, I began to glimpse a kaleidoscope of patterns and possibilities that I had never noticed before. The more I explored the Bible, the more problems I discovered in the Bible. And yet, I also began to see that none of these problems completely eclipsed the most essential claims of Christian faith.

A few months later—not all at once but almost imperceptibly, like a morning walk that begins in starlight but ends in sunlight, and you can't recall exactly when it was that dawn drained the darkness from the sky—a tiny shoot of faith burst anew through the surface of my consciousness. This new faith seemed to have developed from a genus and species that was entirely different from any faith I had known before. Though I had abandoned much of what I had been taught, I found there were some claims that I now trusted more strongly than ever, but I believed these truths in a different way on the basis of an entirely different foundation.

FAITH, FACTS, AND EVIDENCE

Today, three decades after I read Bertrand Russell's *Why I Am Not a Christian* for the first time, I embrace many of the truths that I struggled to believe during that year or two of doubt as well as some beliefs that I never even knew when I began that journey. I believe in a divine Messiah who drew his first ragged breath between a virgin's knees, a wandering teacher who called his followers to seek justice for the marginalized and to identify with the oppressed, a crucified Jew who checked out of his own tomb alive and well, and a risen King who commissioned his followers to proclaim the good news of his kingdom in every nation. I believe the prophecies that point forward to him in the Old Testament and the recollections about him that fill the New Testament. I believe that God will one day re-create this world and flood every crevasse and crest of the cosmos with equity and justice. I believe that the Bible—as it was originally written and intended to be read—tells the truth. I do not accept any of these claims blindly. I am fully aware that I and billions of others around the globe might be wrong, and there are moments when I feel the weight of this possibility more strongly than others. Yet the deeper I've delved into the claims of Scripture, the more I've come to believe that this faith makes the best sense of the evidence.

To some, it may sound strange to mention *evidence* in the same context as *faith*. In the minds of many people—and perhaps you would count yourself among them—faith stands in opposition to evidence. 'Faith is,' atheist writer Christopher Hitchens once declared, 'the surrender of the mind; it's the surrender of reason.' According to Richard Dawkins, 'faith is a state of mind that leads people to believe something—it doesn't matter what—in the total absence of supporting evidence. ... Evidence is explicitly eschewed.' In an address to the Edinburgh International Science Festival, Dawkins went further and referred to faith as 'the great excuse to evade the need to think and evaluate evidence.' Bestselling biologist Jerry Coyne echoes this perspective and describes faith as 'the acceptance of things for which there is no strong evidence.'[8]

---

8   Christopher Hitchens, 'Holier Than Thou', *Penn and Teller: Bullshit!* (May 23, 2005); Richard Dawkins, *The Selfish Gene* (Oxford: Oxford University Press, 1989), 330; Richard Dawkins, 'Address at International Science Festival' (address, Edinburgh, Scotland, 1992); Jerry Coyne, *Faith versus Fact* (New York: Penguin, 2015), 207-8. See also Julian Baggini, *Atheism* (Oxford: Oxford University Press, 2003), 32.

These definitions, however, completely misconstrue the nature and function of faith. I don't deny that it is possible to find people for whom blind religiosity stands as a substitute for evidence. But what such blind religiosity reveals is a deficiency in these believers' understanding and practice of faith, not in faith itself. What Dawkins and others have done is to turn this deficiency into a definition. In the process, they have distorted the meaning and implications of the very word 'faith'.

Faith, at least as understood in the Christian tradition, has never stood in opposition to evidence—and it certainly doesn't eliminate the need for evidence. Faith is a disposition of trust that *includes* evidence. Faced with new facts, faith can even adapt and change to accommodate stronger evidence and better explanations. Augustine of Hippo, one of the most significant thinkers in the first four centuries of Christian history, put it this way: 'You are deeply deceived if you think that we believe in Christ without any proofs.'[9] A more recent theologian has pointed out that faith 'commences with the conviction of the mind based on adequate evidence. ... It is ... not blind but intelligent.'[10]

---

9   Augustine of Hippo, *De fide rerum quae non videntur,* 5. Faith assents to what is unseen but the unseenness of an alleged reality does not negate the possibility that this alleged reality is real, nor does it negate the possibility of evidence for this alleged reality.

10 W.H. Griffith Thomas, *The Principles of Theology* (London: Longmans, 1930), xviii-xix.

Faith in the truthfulness of the Bible may entail more than mere evidence, but it certainly includes no less.

So how can Dawkins, Coyne, and others claim that faith is the acceptance of claims for which there is no supporting evidence?

Such claims from Hitchens and Dawkins and Coyne are possible in part because these individuals have focused their understanding of 'evidence' exclusively on patterns and claims that are subject to scientific tests and hypotheses. When it comes to the evidence for what ought to be accepted as 'real', the only evidences that are admissible in their approach are *empirical* evidences—which is to say, evidences that can be accessed through the five senses and assessed through scientific methods.[11]

I don't wish to dismiss the importance of scientific evidences. When dealing with testable hypotheses, scientific methods are wonderfully useful and generally reliable. Every time I take one of my children to a medical clinic

---

11   According to Jerry Coyne, '*Religious claims are empirical hypotheses.* ... Most religions make claims about what is true in our universe— that is, empirical claims.' *Faith versus Fact*, 23, emphasis in the original. Here, Coyne either confuses or conflates *empirical* (which has to do with realities accessible through human senses) with *ontological* (which has to do with existence). Coyne implicitly suggests that only empirically-verifiable claims should be accepted as true, but this suggestion fails to meet the standard that Coyne himself sets, because there is no empirical evidence to prove his claim that one should only assent to empirically-verifiable claims.

and head to the pharmacy with a prescription, I am entrusting the wellbeing of one of the people I cherish most to pharmaceutical substances that have been subjected to repeatable scientific tests. Antibiotics and black holes and red dwarfs, a heliocentric universe and natural selection and the double helixes of DNA—all of this knowledge comes to us courtesy of scientific observations and calculations. Significant problems emerge, though, whenever scientific evidences become the standard by which we assess every aspect of knowledge. One of the most significant problems with limiting our range of evidence to such realities is that few past events leave behind evidence that can be assessed by purely scientific means.

To gain a clearer glimpse of this problem, meet me in the parking lot outside my office in the city of Louisville. Let's take a road trip together to a natural spring at the base of a hill in central Kentucky, an hour or so south of my house.

What if Abraham Lincoln was born in Liechtenstein?

Louisville is a river city, founded on the banks of the Ohio River and stretching twenty miles south of the river. I live and work in an older section of the city; here, century-old brick houses are packed tightly amid towering oaks and maples. It takes a few minutes of driving to reach the highway that leads from the neighborhoods to the suburbs and then to the rural rim of the city. About fifteen miles south of the city limits, the gentle slopes and tussocked valleys of the river basin begin to rumple into tree-thick hills that eventually modulate into the Appalachian Mountains. It was in a cabin nestled near the base of one of these hills that Abraham Lincoln was born.

Or at least that's what people have claimed for more than two centuries.

But how can anyone know beyond any conceivable doubt that Abraham Lincoln was truly born in a cabin along the cusp of this sunken spring?

No strands of Lincoln-family DNA have been plucked from the soil here. The cabin itself is long gone, replaced by a symbolic structure that was assembled sometime after Lincoln's death. The testable artifacts that have been unearthed around this property suggest that cabin-dwellers settled in this spot sometime in the eighteenth century—but there is no scientific evidence here that can prove beyond any possible doubt that this is where Abraham Lincoln was born.

So what about the signs along the interstate that proclaim 'Birthplace of Abraham Lincoln'? What about the millions of people each year who stream down these stone steps into the coolness of the sinking spring, confident that the man who was born near this spot was the one who would end the enslavement of African Americans in the United States? And, if no one can prove empirically that the Great Emancipator was born here, why should we commemorate this place at all? And yet, we *do* commemorate not only this place but also thousands of similar places and stories for which no empirical experiment can provide unquestionable evidence.

Every two or three years, I come to this sinking spring with my two daughters whose melanin-rich skin and tightly-kinked curls reveal the beauty of their African heritage. Here, we recall the magnificent resilience of the African slaves and remember how the baby who was born in this place became the president who set their ancestors free. We hike a nearby creek where Lincoln nearly drowned as a child, and we stop at the spot on the Green River Turnpike where Lincoln first saw African Americans taken south to be sold into slavery. I cannot scientifically demonstrate every detail of the stories that my daughters hear here. I cannot prove beyond any conceivable doubt that Abraham Lincoln was born in Kentucky and not New Hampshire or Canada or Liechtenstein. And yet, there are truths embedded in these stories for which I am ready to risk everything I am and everything I possess.

WHY I HAVE FAITH THAT FINLAND ISN'T FICTIONAL

'There is simply no way,' Jerry Coyne declares as part of his argument for the incompatibility of faith and facts, 'that *any* faith can prove beyond question that its claims are true.'[12] I do not dispute the truth of this declaration—but the dilemma he describes is not unique to claims related to religious faith. What he declares is true of every claim that's grounded in history. It's as true of the nativity of Abraham Lincoln as it is of the nativity of Jesus Christ. It's as true of the military campaigns that took Alexander the Great to India as it is of the death of Elvis Presley, the resurrection of Jesus, the dictation of the Qur'an to Muhammad, and the inscription of the Book of Mormon on plates of gold. Some of these claims are false and some of them are true, but none of them can survive the standards of proof that Dawkins, Coyne, and others like them have demanded. When it comes to events that happened in the past, all of us make choices about our lives—and sometimes about our deaths—based on claims that cannot be empirically verified or scientifically proven. That's why agnostic biblical scholar Bart Ehrman rightly recognizes that 'everybody has faith in something. My agnosticism is a kind of faith.'[13]

The question is not whether or not we have faith but whether there is evidence to support the faith we have. At its worst, faith can be distorted into a blind conviction that lacks supporting evidence. At its best, faith is confidence that's grounded in evidence. In between these two possibilities,

---

12   Coyne, *Faith versus Fact*, 74.

13   Bart Ehrman, quoted in Gary Kamiya, 'Jesus Is Just Alright with Him', *Salon* (April 3, 2009).

there are billions of people who live with mostly reasonable beliefs even though they've never taken the time to gather evidence for those beliefs.

When it comes to the events inscribed in the pages of the Bible, the evidence—like all evidence from ancient history—consists of an uneven chain of texts and artifacts that stretches more than a millennium into the past. Our information about what ancient Christians believed and practiced survives in faded sentences inscribed on parchments and papyri, in etchings on walls of stone, and in paintings formed from multihued minglings of pigments and plaster. The text that manifold millions of Christians trust as the Bible today consists of sixty-six books organized into two collections, the Old Testament and the New Testament—but no original manuscripts of any of these texts survive. They come to us in the form of fragments and manuscripts copied from copies of copies of works originally penned in Hebrew and Aramaic and Greek. The process of reconstructing these pieces to determine what happened in the past is not accomplished primarily through scientific experiments or empirical measurements. History is crafted by constructing scenarios that draw together texts and artifacts to make the most plausible sense of the surviving evidence. If an alleged event happened hundreds or thousands of years ago, much of this evidence must be reconstructed from documents that survive only as copies of long-lost originals.

Such reconstructions can't prove what happened beyond any possible question or doubt—but that's true not only of events that took place in the ancient past but also of more recent happenings. If you don't believe me, search the Internet for information about Barack Obama's birth certificate or the Apollo 11 space flight that landed two men on the moon in 1969. It won't take you long to unearth entire communities of people who claim that former U.S. president Barack Obama was born in Kenya or that Neil Armstrong's moonwalk was faked on a military base or a Hollywood soundstage. And it's not merely anonymous communities on the Internet that make such claims. I had an uncle who went to his grave still claiming that the moon landing was staged in New Mexico. Look hard enough on the Internet and you'll even find a group that denies the existence of Finland. Even when presented with evidence, diehard Finland-deniers always find some detail to doubt about the dominion of the Finns. ('Name one world-famous person from Finland. See? You can't do it!' 'You say you've landed in the airport in Helsinki? Prove to me that the airport isn't actually in Sweden.')

Despite such objections, I remain quite confident that Finland is no fiction. Most likely, you would agree. And yet, the reason I believe there really is a country between Russia and Sweden is not because I can comprehensively counter every conceivable question that anyone might ask about the location of this alleged nation. I believe in the existence of Finland, Neil Armstrong's moonwalk, the Hawaiian nativity of the forty-fourth president of the United States, and the birth of the sixteenth president in Kentucky because texts and artifacts and other evidences have produced a certain plausibility when it comes to these realities. None of these claims can be proven beyond every conceivable question or doubt, and each one requires some measure of faith—but it is faith that is grounded in evidence.

'THE BEST CURE ... COULD ONE BUT TAKE IT ACCORDING TO THE TRUTH'

Down the hill from the spot where Abraham Lincoln's first cries rang out among the red maple trees, there is a tiny museum dedicated to the memory of Lincoln's early years in Kentucky. In one hall of the museum there is a book protected by a pane of glass. It is the Lincoln family Bible. This particular copy of the King James Bible was one of the first books that young Abraham Lincoln learned to read.

The words of this Bible shaped Lincoln's sense of justice and seeped into almost every speech that he wrote. Yet, particularly during the years that he worked as a lawyer and a senator, Lincoln could not bring himself to believe that this book was wholly true. The Bible—Lincoln wrote in 1841 to a friend who resided in Louisville—would be 'the best cure for the "blues" could one but take it according to the truth.'[14] I don't know whether or not Lincoln was right about the Bible being the best cure for the blues. I do believe, however, that the book behind the glass at Lincoln's birthplace can be taken 'according to the truth'.

When I say that the words in this particular Bible can be taken 'according to the truth', I'm not suggesting that there are no translation errors or textual incongruities within its pages. There are textual and translational problems in every version of the Bible, and this particular printing of the King James Bible is no exception. Nevertheless, the sentences printed in this book are, for the most part, faithful renderings of copies of Hebrew, Aramaic, and Greek texts that preserved the biblical texts with reasonable accuracy. Not one of these ancient copies is perfect, but they were reproduced with sufficient precision to recover the intended meaning of the texts that eventually made their way into the Bible.

The Bible does not come with empirical proof and it certainly does not come without problems—but it also does not come without evidence. The evidences for the trustworthiness of this text are not scientific but historical. Such evidences do not result in the same type of certainty as scientific experiments or mathematical calculations. What historical evidences provide instead is a reasonable confidence

---

14   Abraham Lincoln, letter to Mary Speed, September 27, 1841.

that grows from reconstructions that are cultivated in a seedbed of testimonies and texts, monuments and artifacts.

I don't pretend to be able to prove every claim imprinted in the pages of the Bible—but neither can I prove everything I believe about the military campaigns of Alexander the Great, the birth of Abraham Lincoln, or the module from Apollo 11 that made it to the moon. Nevertheless, there is evidence that supports the reality of each of these events. This evidence has produced a strong plausibility that has led me to a reasonable sense of confidence when it comes to my beliefs about them. The same is true when it comes to the Bible.

A PATHWAY TO PLAUSIBILITY

The Bible is a tough book to believe, and there are people who blindly accept what it has to say without considering the difficulties. At the same time, there are also people who have struggled deeply with what the Bible has to say and still find substantive reasons to sustain their trust in these texts. Throughout the remainder of this book, I'll be exploring a few of the reasons why it is far from irrational to trust the text of Scripture.

When you reach the final chapter of this book, you may decide that these evidences are compelling, or you may conclude that they're still not enough. If you remain unconvinced, I won't be surprised, and I won't think anything less of you. I enjoy the friendship of several highly intelligent atheists who have studied nearly as many texts defending the Bible as I have. Even after reading these books, they still find the God of the Bible to be slightly less believable than the Tooth Fairy. Their continuing atheism reveals that the factors that make faith plausible are more complex than any single book can address by itself—but, once again, that's true of almost any expression of belief or disbelief.

The doubts and the convictions that work together within us to form what we believe are too complex to be reduced to a single text in isolation from everything else. It's never a single book or idea that crushes faith or creates it. It's the loneliness of that first year of college entwined with the recognition that the people you trusted most told you lies about God. It's that one coincidence that you can't quite explain coupled with a community that kept caring for you even when everyone else turned away. It's the knowing nod of that one professor who listened to your questions even when no one else would take the time. It's a book or a blog post or a conversation that entwines itself with the point of your deepest pain. It's all of this, coupled with a vast tangle of other threads of which you're not even consciously aware. Sometimes, these storylines lead you to a faith that includes the divine. Other times, they lead to an expression of faith that tries its best to leave God behind. And yet, none of these storylines operates alone, separated from all the other strands of your life.

Beneath this multitude of human factors, I also happen to believe that, whenever someone embraces truth in the pages of Scripture, it's a result of God working to reveal his truth. You may disagree with me on that point, but my goal isn't to convince you to agree with me about everything I believe. What I want to do is simply to sketch out one possible pathway that a reasonable person might take that would lead him or her to trust that the Bible is true. There's more than one way to make that case, but I'll only be exploring a couple of those ways in this book. If the pathway I sketch in these pages doesn't convince you, I'm still glad that you've joined me on this journey. If this book turns out to be one of the many threads that leads you someday to delight in Jesus, all the better.

Yes, the Bible is a difficult book to believe. And yet, after decades of study mingled with both faith and doubt, I've become convinced that it is not unreasonable to trust the texts that make up this book. When these documents are understood in the ways they were written to be read, there is an intellectually robust case to be made that these texts tell the truth. The way that I've chosen to begin developing this case here is by examining the New Testament Gospels and then by considering what it might mean for the rest of the Bible if the story that these texts tell turns out to be plausible.

RECOMMENDED RESOURCES

Lewis, C.S. *Surprised by Joy.* (New York: Harcourt Brace, 1955).

McGrath, Alister. *Dawkins' God.* 2nd edition. (West Sussex: Wiley, 2015).

McGrath, Alister. *Surprised by Meaning.* (Louisville: Westminster John Knox, 2011).

Meek, Esther. *Longing to Know.* (Chicago: Brazos Press, 2003).

Plantinga, Alvin. *Knowledge and Christian Belief.* (Grand Rapids: Eerdmans, 2015).

2

Were the Gospels Written to Tell What Happened in History?

I like atheists.

That's partly because most atheists I've met are willing to consider the evidences for Christianity, even if they find faith in Jesus and faith in a Flying Spaghetti Monster to be equally preposterous. And so, when the Society of Secular Students at the University of Louisville invited me to participate in a dialogue about the resurrection of Jesus, I was eager to accept.

When the dialogue began, I was one of only two Christians in a room packed with a combination of curious skeptics and convinced atheists. The question-and-answer session that followed my presentation was scheduled for thirty minutes, but it ended up lasting almost three hours. Before it was over, we had discussed not only the resurrection of Jesus but also how ethics derived from the teachings of

Jesus have influenced religious freedom, human rights, and the abolition of slavery. Near the end of the dialogue, one last student made his way to the microphone at the front of the room.

'I'm an engineering major,' he said. 'When I'm making my calculations, all that matters is getting an answer that works here and now, in this life. It doesn't matter what happened one thousand or two thousand years ago. But I actually like a lot of what you're saying about Christianity. What I want to know is this: Is there any way that I can be a Christian without believing that Jesus really showed up in history or that he was raised from the dead?'

What this student wanted was the same thing that I've found myself desiring from time to time. Sometimes, it seems like it would be easier to embrace some form of faith that doesn't require me to face the awkwardness of Jesus in history. It would be simpler, in some ways, not to have to consider whether the stone-cold corpse of a crucified rabble-rouser somehow metamorphosed into a living soul two thousand years ago. And so, what I wanted to say at first to this engineering student was, 'Certainly! Don't worry about the weirdness of miracles or resurrections or a virgin conception. You can trust Jesus without believing any of these events happened. Just do the best you can to follow the teachings of Jesus, and everything will be fine.'

But that's not what I said, because I don't believe it's true.

What I said instead was something like this: 'Everything in the Christian faith depends on this one truth: that God himself entered history as a human being who lived and died and rose from the dead. If this event didn't happen in real life, nothing else about Christianity matters. There is no Christianity worth believing unless Jesus was raised from the dead.' It was difficult for me to speak those words, but I still believe they're true.

There is no Christianity worth believing unless something supernatural intersected history in the person of Jesus. If Jesus never lived at all or if he died and stayed dead, there's no good reason to consider whether anyone ought to live their life according to anything he was supposed to have said. There's certainly no reason to waste your time wrestling with the dilemma of whether or not the Bible might be true. If the flesh of Jesus decayed into dust, the texts that preserve stories about him are nothing more than a hodgepodge of ancient tales that have—due to a random series of fortuitous coincidences—managed to transform the course of human history.

That's why I've selected the New Testament Gospels—some of the earliest surviving testimonies about Jesus—as the starting point for this journey. If historical and literary examinations of these texts suggest that what they claim about Jesus might be plausible, it's worth considering what that might mean for the rest of the Bible. The mere plausibility of these testimonies cannot, of course, sustain the claim that the Bible as a whole is trustworthy. It does, however, provide a starting place from which we can consider whether trusting the Bible is even an option for people who want to ground their beliefs in evidence.[1]

In case you're not familiar with the New Testament, when I refer to 'New Testament Gospels', what I'm describing are the first four books in the New Testament. These four compositions are known by the names Matthew, Mark, Luke, and John. Scholars disagree when it comes to the question of who actually wrote these books. Virtually every biblical scholar—whether or not they believe what the

---

1   The methodological approach of this book is one that I have termed 'verificationalist presuppositionalism.' In this approach, a fundamental distinction in the cognitive sphere between those who presuppose the being of God and those who do not is recognized; at the same time, it is also recognized that this distinction does not negate apologetics on the basis of common notions nor does it exclude shared observations or sensory experiences that may provide bases for meaningful dialogue between believers and non-believers, resulting in the confirmation or disconfirmation of hypotheses on the basis of plausibility and verifiability. Francis Schaeffer's approach similarly brought together verificationalism with the recognition of a cognitive distinction between believers and unbelievers. For discussions of Schaeffer's approach, see Scott Burson and Jerry Walls, *C.S. Lewis and Francis Schaeffer* (Downers Grove: InterVarsity, 2009); E.R. Geehan, 'The "Presuppositional" Apologetic of Francis Schaeffer', *Themelios* 9 (1972), 10-18; Gordon Lewis, 'Schaeffer's Apologetic Method', in *Reflections on Francis Schaeffer,* ed. Ronald Ruegsegger (Grand Rapids: Zondervan, 1986), 69-104.

Gospels have to say about Jesus—agrees, however, that this quartet of texts was written in the second half of the first century A.D., give or take a few years.

A POINT ON WHICH WE CAN AGREE

At this point, I'm not suggesting that these texts are divinely inspired or even necessarily true. If I started out by assuming the truth of the Gospels, the result would be a circular argument that begs every question I'm hoping to answer. My starting point is, instead, a single fact on which we can both agree: the texts included in the New Testament preserve claims about Jesus that circulated among readers and hearers in the ancient Roman Empire. The claims in these texts may be false or they may be true. They may be the ravings of lunatics or they may be the words of God— but the Gospels and early Christian letters are, at the very least, a collection of ancient testimonies. These texts may turn out to be something more than ancient claims about Jesus, but they are certainly no less. After years of examining these compositions in some of the same ways that I might examine other ancient texts, there are a few conclusions that I've found difficult to avoid. Throughout this chapter and the next one, I'll be carefully exploring each one of these conclusions:

- The authors of the New Testament Gospels intended their compositions to be received as testimonies about events that actually happened.
- The accounts that were brought together to form the Gospels originated in the times and places where the alleged events happened.
- The testimonies in the New Testament Gospels can be traced back to eyewitnesses and persons who were closely associated with eyewitnesses.
- When these accounts about Jesus were written down, persons who claimed to have witnessed the alleged events were still alive and available to correct misrepresentations of their experiences.

These conclusions form the foundations for why I find the claims about Jesus in the New Testament to be historically plausible. I do not embrace these conclusions on the basis of wishful thinking or blind faith. These conclusions are grounded in textual and cultural artifacts from which a broad range of historical possibilities can be plausibly reconstructed. Throughout the next couple of chapters, my goal is simply to consider whether or not these conclusions are warranted by the artifacts and the evidence.

In the end, the reconstruction of evidence that I find most plausible is one in which a miracle-performing Jewish prophet was crucified and then returned to life almost two thousand years ago. This isn't the only possible reconstruction of the evidence, and I'm fully aware that not everyone will be convinced by the evidences that have brought me to this place. But, then again, not everyone on this planet finds the evidence for Neil Armstrong's lunar landing or the Hawaiian birth of Barack Obama to be compelling either. No belief about any past event stands beyond every conceivable doubt. Since past events have—by definition—*passed,* these events cannot be scientifically re-created or replicated in a laboratory. And yet, simply because it is possible to doubt the evidence does not mean that there is an absence of evidence. That's why it's unreasonable to assert—as Jerry Coyne does in his book *Faith versus Fact*—that religious assertions require 'the acceptance of things for which there is no strong evidence.'[2] The claims that Christians make about the Gospels may be true or they may be false, but these beliefs have not emerged without significant evidence.

DID THE AUTHORS OF THE NEW TESTAMENT INTEND TO WRITE ABOUT REAL EVENTS?

Before exploring specific texts and artifacts related to the Gospels, there is a far more basic question that should be considered, however: *Were the testimonies preserved about Jesus in the New Testament Gospels intended to be taken as descriptions of real events in the first place?* It is possible, after

---

2   Coyne, *Faith versus Fact*, 207-8.

all, that the Gospels that came to be included in the New Testament were never meant to describe actual occurrences. Perhaps they were written as fiction, but later readers have misconstrued them as fact. That's what several scholars of religion have suggested over the years. According to Reza Aslan's bestselling book *Zealot,* for example, the New Testament Gospels 'are not, nor were they ever meant to be, a historical documentation of Jesus's life. They are testimonies of faith composed by communities of faith and written many years after the events they describe.'[3]

Reza Aslan is correct that the Gospels were most likely composed decades after the events they narrate—but so were the most reliable surviving accounts of the life of Emperor Nero.[4] The writing of biographies didn't occur nearly as quickly in the ancient world as it does in the modern era. As long as information from eyewitnesses was accessible, an accurate and widely-accepted biography could still be constructed many years after the events occurred.

---

3   Reza Aslan, *Zealot* (New York: Random House, 2013), xxvi.

4   Josephus mentioned Emperor Nero in *Bellum Judaicum,* books 2–6, almost thirty years after the emperor's death but no biography of Nero. Around 117 A.D. Cornelius Tacitus summarized the life of Nero in *Annales,* books 13–16, approximately fifty years after the emperor's death. Of course, other records and chronicles related to Nero preceded the compositions of Josephus and Tacitus which may not have survived; however, the same might be said regarding Jesus in light of the reference in Luke's Gospel to 'many' narratives about Jesus prior to this particular Gospel (Luke 1:1).

Despite Aslan's assertion to the contrary, the Gospels don't fail the test of providing 'historical documentation' simply because they are 'testimonies of faith'. No one denies that the earliest records of the life of Jesus were based on the testimonies of women and men who had committed themselves to follow Jesus—but a text doesn't become unhistorical simply because it happens to be a testimony of faith. The crucial question isn't whether the testimonies of believers in Jesus were the sources behind these texts—of course they were! The question is, 'Did their testimonies describe events that actually happened? And were the texts that preserve these testimonies intended to recount real events?' If the most comprehensive accounts of the life of Jesus were never intended to provide us with historical testimony, any further discussion about the resurrection of Jesus or the trustworthiness of the Bible is pointless. And so, before going any further, I want to explore the question of whether or not the authors of the New Testament Gospels intended to tell their readers what really happened in the first place.

WHAT ARE THE GOSPELS?

This dilemma is, in part, a question about the *genre* of the Gospels. The word 'genre' describes a category into which a particular culture places an artistic or literary composition. The reason a piece of art or literature lands in a particular category is because it shares certain key features with other compositions in that category. The genre of a literary composition is one of many factors that influences whether we receive a particular testimony as fiction or fact.

Sometimes, the genre of an artistic or literary artifact is so obvious to us that we don't even think about it. If you're holding a book that begins with the words, 'Once upon a time,' you sense immediately that you're probably not reading a manual about composting or birdwatching or automobile maintenance. If the first phrase that splashes across the screen at the cinema is, 'A long time ago in a galaxy far far away,' it's more likely that you're about to see a space fantasy than a documentary about the Galápagos Islands.

Other times, however, the genre is less obvious. That's partly because writers may sometimes blend genres in ways that make it difficult to separate fact from fiction. Consider, for example, a film like *Forrest Gump* where the biography of a character who never existed is woven into the lives of famous figures like Elvis Presley and Lyndon Johnson. Or what about the bestselling novel *Abraham Lincoln: Vampire Hunter*? This book begins with words from the real-life Lincoln but then repaints the great emancipator as the greatest vampire killer of all time. And where in this continuum does a film like Walt Disney's classic animated retelling of *Robin Hood* fit? King Richard and Prince John were real-life rulers of England in the twelfth century, but they show up in this film as talking felines. Historical people and places and events provide the framework for such works, but the creators clearly never meant their compositions to be taken as pure historical fact.

So what about the genre of the New Testament Gospels? What types of texts are these first four compositions in the New Testament? And how should this shape the ways that we read them?

When the Gospels are compared with other ancient texts, the Gospels fall within an ancient literary genre known as *bios,* a Greek word that simply means 'life'. The word *bios* is sometimes translated as 'biography', but the category of Greco-Roman *bios* was quite a bit broader than what you might find beneath the sign that reads 'Biographies' at your local library. The *bios* genre did include meticulously-researched Greek and Latin biographies like the volumes that flowed from the pens of Plutarch, Suetonius, and Tacitus—but formal biographies of this sort weren't the only types of texts that fell within the *bios* genre. The genre of ancient biography could also encompass compositions that were closer to *Abraham Lincoln: Vampire Hunter* than to anything a classical author might have composed for the upper echelons of Athens or Rome.

To understand the breadth of the *bios* genre, let's take a look at one of the most popular ancient novelistic biographies, the *Life of Alexander*. This romanticized biography spices up the real life of Alexander the Great with a string of fabulous but mostly made-up anecdotes. According to this *bios,* Alexander's birthfather wasn't Philip of Macedon but the last pharaoh of Egypt assisted by the god Amun. As a teenager, Alexander tamed a warhorse that had once consumed human beings. As king, he stood before a sea in Cilicia, and the wind and waves bowed before him. Unlike more formal biographers, the authors of novelistic biographies tended to write as anonymous third-person narrators, and they freely borrowed from a wide range of earlier compositions without explicitly identifying their sources.

ARE THE NEW TESTAMENT GOSPELS MORE FICTION THAN FACT?

So what does all of this have to do with the claims made in the New Testament Gospels? *In some ways, the Gospels are more similar to ancient novelistic biographies than any other type of text.* Apart from the opening verses of Luke's Gospel, everything in the New Testament Gospels is conveyed from the perspective of a third-person narrator, and the authors never explicitly identify themselves by name. What's more, Matthew's and Luke's Gospels incorporate more than two-thirds of the Gospel According to Mark without ever mentioning where this content came from— much like the novelistic biographies which were narrated in the third person and which freely borrowed from earlier writings without identifying their sources. Taken together, these patterns and others suggest significant similarities between the New Testament Gospels and ancient novelistic biographies.[5]

These similarities represent a potential quandary for those who believe that the Gospels were composed to convey historical testimony. Do the similarities between the New Testament Gospels and novelistic biographies suggest that the resurrected Jesus is as fictional as the exaggerated Alexander described in the *Life of Alexander*? And why—if the Gospels are so similar to ancient novelistic biographies—should anyone take the resurrection of Jesus and other miracles in the Gospels to be anything other than pious exaggerations? Such a dilemma deserves serious attention. And so, before exploring how the Gospels provide a foundation for trusting the Bible as a whole, I want to look together at a couple of reasons why the Gospels seem to be describing real events,

---

5   Klaus Berger has identified four primary categories within the *bios* genre: (1) encomial biographies modeled after speeches given in honor of an individual at death; (2) peripatetic biographies that presented a subject's life chronologically; (3) Alexandrian biographies that presented a subject's life topically and systematically; (4) popular-novelistic biographies written to inform popular audiences about the individual in an entertaining way. See Klaus Berger, 'Hellenistische Gattungen im Neuen Testament', in *Aufstieg und Niedergang der römischen Welt* II, 25 (1984), 197-8. The New Testament Gospels exhibit some affinities with popular-novelistic biographies; however, similarities may also be observed between the Gospels and the Alexandrian and peripatetic biographical types.

even if they exhibit some of the same literary features as novelistic biographies.

1. THE MOST FANTASTIC CLAIMS IN THE GOSPELS ARE CORROBORATED IN ANOTHER GENRE:

One reason why I'm convinced that the Gospel authors didn't intend to write fiction is because *the most crucial claims that the authors of the Gospels made about Jesus also appear in another literary genre, the genre of epistle.* Much of the New Testament is made up of epistles—letters sent to particular communities to be read publicly and then circulated widely. Many of these epistles were penned prior to the New Testament Gospels. Most important for our purposes, virtually every essential claim about Jesus that appears in the Gospels also shows up in these letters, despite the fact that these epistles were composed for people who already knew about Jesus.

The New Testament epistles corroborate, at the very least, the following claims from the Gospels:

- Jesus was physically born into a Jewish family that traced its lineage back to King David (Rom. 1:3; Gal. 4:4; compare Matt. 1:1).
- Jesus had twelve close followers as well as relatives who were well known among early Christians (1 Cor. 9:5; 15:5; compare Matt. 10:1-4; 13:55-56).

- Jesus was sentenced to death during the political administration of Pontius Pilate (1 Tim. 6:13; compare Mark 15:1-15).
- Jesus was crucified, buried, and raised from the dead (1 Cor. 1:22-23; 2:8; 15:3-4; 1 Pet. 1:3, 21, and many other texts; compare Mark 15:16–16:8).
- Jesus was seen alive on the third day after his death (1 Cor. 15:3-6; compare Matt. 17:23; 28:1-10); he later ascended from human sight (1 Tim. 3:16; compare Luke 24:50).

It's at this point that one of the clearest distinctions emerges between the New Testament Gospels and novelistic biographies like *Life of Alexander*. No one today believes that Alexander the Great was fathered by a pharaoh or that he rode a horse that once consumed human flesh. This disbelief is not, however, based merely on the fact that these claims stand outside usual human experience or because they sound outlandish to us today. If you decided to disbelieve anything about the past that sounds absurd, you would end up repudiating the reality of many bizarre events that actually happened. You'd probably reject the dancing plague of 1518, for example, as well as the cloud of darkness that settled in the skies over Europe and Asia Minor for an entire year in 536 A.D.—despite the fact that both of these are well-attested historical events.[6] The claims in *Life of Alexander* are implausible for far more objective reasons than the mere fact that they sound outlandish. One of these reasons is that *the most fantastic claims made in the novelistic retellings of Alexander's life are not corroborated in the reports about him in other literary texts and genres.*

When it comes to Jesus, however, the most fantastic claim of all—the declaration that Jesus walked out of a tomb alive on the third day after his death—is repeated in a range of other genres, including the genre of epistle. The fact that certain claims about the life of Jesus and his resurrection are attested in more than one genre doesn't prove that the events took place. The presence of the same affirmations in two distinct genres does suggest, however, that early Christians probably didn't intend these claims to be read as fiction.

2. THE GOSPELS WERE WRITTEN IN A NOVELISTIC STYLE BECAUSE THEY WERE MEANT TO REACH A BROADER AUDIENCE THAN FORMAL BIOGRAPHIES:

Here's the primary reason why I'm convinced that the authors of the Gospels were intent on recounting real events: *the style and structure selected by the authors of the Gospels had more to do with their intended audiences than*

---

6   M.G.L. Baillie, 'Dendrochronology Raises Questions about the Nature of the A.D. 536 Dust-Veil Event', in *Holocene* 4 (1994), 212-17; John Waller, *The Dancing Plague* (Naperville: Sourcebooks, 2009).

with the historicity of their claims. Ancient biographers—no less than writers today—chose the styles and structures for their compositions based in part on their target audiences. Ancient texts that were intended to reach the broadest possible audiences could be penned in a simple and episodic style, unburdened by explicit references to sources—which is precisely what we see in the Gospels.

More often than not, compositions in this class were fictional, but not necessarily and not always. Based both on internal claims in the Gospels and on external corroborations of their claims in other genres, it seems that the New Testament Gospels were composed like novelistic biographies because *they were being produced for a broad and diverse range of people.* Simply put, the Gospels were intended to be accessible and meaningful not only to the literary elite but also to popular audiences.[7]

---

7   One other reason why the Gospels freely incorporated earlier sources of information about the life of Jesus and didn't explicitly mention their authors is probably because that's how the historical books in the Old Testament were written. The Old Testament historical texts—books like Kings and Chronicles and Ruth—drew from earlier sources and never referenced their authors by name. The composers of the first Gospels seem to have mimicked this pattern. This pattern suggests that the Gospel writers intended their compositions to be read in continuity with Old Testament historical texts, which they read as descriptions of real events. See Armin Baum, 'The Anonymity of the New Testament History Books', in *Novum Testamentum* (2008), 128, 133-4, 137-9.

Even today, the style of a text doesn't necessarily determine whether the composition is fact or fiction. A few weeks ago, one of my colleagues finished his doctoral dissertation; the focus of his dissertation was Phillis Wheatley, the first African-American poet ever to have her compositions published.[8] This dissertation included hundreds of footnotes—but there was not a single picture to be found in the entire project and there were only a few anecdotes. While reading his dissertation, it occurred to me that my younger children had never read about Phillis Wheatley. And so, after I read the dissertation, I headed to a used bookstore and located a children's biography about this historical heroine.

The book about Phillis Wheatley that I found in the bookstore was written in simple language interspersed with dozens of pictures and stories—but there was not a single footnote in the entire book. In some ways, this children's biography reads more like a novel than a historical textbook. And yet, the text that my daughter is reading about Phillis Wheatley is no less factual than my friend's doctoral dissertation; my daughter's book is simply aimed at a different audience. My friend wrote his dissertation to prove he deserves an academic doctorate, and his dissertation was perfect for that purpose. His dissertation is, however, far from

---

8   Curtis Woods, 'The Literary Reception of the Spirituality of Phillis Wheatley (1753-1784): an Afrosensitive Reading' (Ph.D. dissertation, The Southern Baptist Theological Seminary, 2018).

perfect for my ten-year-old! No matter how much Phillis Wheatley might interest my daughter, she would never make it past the first chapter of his doctoral dissertation. And yet, it will take her less than a day to master the biography that I purchased to deepen her pride in her African heritage by introducing her to the life of Phillis Wheatley. The novelistic style isn't what determines whether or not this biography of Phillis Wheatley tells the truth. What the style of this biography reveals is the audience that the author intended to address. Claiming that the New Testament Gospels are fictional simply because they are similar to ancient novelistic biographies would be like declaring that my daughter's biography of Phillis Wheatley is false because it's written as a series of anecdotes and lacks any footnotes.

Early Christians may have been right about Jesus or they may have been wrong, but this much is clear: they were convinced that the proclamation of Jesus ought to reach people from every ethnic and social demographic (Matt. 28:19; Luke 24:47). As a result, the stories of Jesus were never recorded in formal biographies whose audiences would be limited to the uppermost echelons of Roman culture. Instead, the earliest stories about Jesus were shaped and edited into intricate yet simple biographies that never explicitly named their sources or their authors. This approach resulted in texts that read a lot like ancient novelistic biographies—but that doesn't mean these texts are fictitious. The most appropriate style and structure for such a broad audience was a popular style, which turns out to have been a style similar to ancient historical novels.[9]

The opening lines of the Gospel ascribed to Luke link the author's narrative to 'those who from the beginning were eyewitnesses' (Luke 1:2). The author of the Gospel According to John made a similar point when he wrote regarding his account of the crucifixion: 'He who saw this has testified so that you also may believe. His testimony is true, and he knows that he tells the truth' (John 19:35). Real similarities do exist between the New Testament Gospels and ancient novels, but there's nothing quite like these affirmations of eyewitness testimony in any novelistic biography such as *Life of Alexander*. Whether or not the Gospels accurately describe what happened in the life of Jesus, claims like these suggest that the Gospel authors never intended their words to be read as fiction.

DID THE AUTHORS OF THE GOSPELS INTEND TO WRITE FICTION OR FACT?

Still, some religious scholars continue to treat the Gospels as narratives that were intended to be read as symbolic

---

9   Justin Marc Smith focused his genre analysis less on compositional features and more on the intended audience. He identified the Gospels as 'contemporary open biographies'—that is to say, works written in the lifetimes of the eyewitnesses and intended for a broad, open audience. See Justin Marc Smith, *Why Bios?* (London: T&T Clark, 2015), 218-20.

fiction. In an interview published in *The New York Times*, the president of Union Theological Seminary declared that it doesn't matter whether or not the resurrection took place, because the Gospels were never meant to tell what happened in history. 'The message of Easter,' she claims,

> is that love is stronger than life or death. ... For Christians for whom the physical resurrection becomes a sort of obsession, that seems to me to be a pretty wobbly faith. What if tomorrow someone found the body of Jesus still in the tomb? Would that then mean that Christianity was a lie? No, faith is stronger than that.[10]

In the mind of this scholar, the central truth declared through the life of Jesus has nothing to do with any event that happened in history. The entire meaning of the resurrection stories is simply that 'love is stronger than life or death'—which sounds more like the contents of a fortune cookie than it does like anything you might actually read in the New Testament.

The stories of Jesus in the Gospels could be the culmination of an elaborate hoax, they might be the conclusion of a long and twisted series of misunderstandings, or they may have been woven together from testimonies that can be traced

10 Nicholas Kristof, 'Reverend, You Say the Virgin Birth Is "a Bizarre Claim"?' *The New York Times* (April 20, 2019), https://www.nytimes.com/2019/04/20/opinion/sunday/christian-easter-serene-jones.html

back to eyewitnesses. The Jesus depicted in the Gospels may have been a legend or he may be the Lord, but he cannot be reasonably reduced to a mere symbol of how strong love can be. This may seem like 'pretty wobbly faith' to some, but this was the faith that sustained the Christians who composed the New Testament texts and who gave up their lives refusing to worship any deity apart from Jesus. This recognition that the authors of the Gospels meant to make claims about real events eliminates the ridiculous notion that the Gospels should be seen merely as sources of inspiration, stripped of the weirdness of miracles and resurrections and ascensions into the sky. There is no way to believe in Jesus as he is presented in the Gospels without also embracing the sheer strangeness of these claims. If God's mighty works never happened in history or if the body of Jesus never exited the tomb, there is no faith in Jesus worth believing or receiving.

All of this brings us to a crucial dilemma when it comes to whether or not the Bible should be trusted: When we examine the New Testament Gospels in the same way that we might explore other ancient compositions, can the testimonies in these texts be traced back to reliable sources? That's the question that will be our focus in the next chapter.

RECOMMENDED RESOURCES

Bauckham, Richard (ed.). *The Gospels for All Christians.* (Grand Rapids: Eerdmans, 1997).

Burridge, Richard. *What Are the Gospels?* 2nd edition. (Waco: Baylor University Press, 2018).

Keener, Craig. *Christobiography.* (Grand Rapids: Eerdmans, 2019).

Klink, Edward, III (ed.). *The Audience of the Gospels.* 3rd edition. (London: T&T Clark, 2010).

Smith, Justin Marc. *Why Bios?* (London: T&T Clark, 2015).

3

Are the Gospels Historically Plausible?

Sometimes, truth really is stranger than fiction.

In 1876, about a hundred miles east of where I live today, a grandmother was making lye soap on her front porch. Suddenly, an odd series of thuds in the field beside her house interrupted the silence of her labors, and she sent her grandson to see what was happening. Her grandson claimed it was snowing, but the weather was too warm and too clear for snow. And so, Mrs Crouch stepped off the porch to see for herself.

What the grandmother saw when she walked across the field still sounds unbelievable today.

Scraps of raw meat were raining from a cloudless sky.

PLAUSIBILITY, HISTORY, AND MEAT FROM THE SKY

If you cruise down the rural roads that crisscross Bath County, Kentucky today, you probably won't notice anything unusual, except perhaps the creek and the road that are both named 'Mud Lick'—which sounds strange enough until you learn that Mud Lick Road intersects with Elk Lick Road southeast of Big Bone Lick Road about eight miles southwest of the community of Salt Lick. And yet, on March 3, 1876, a spot near Mud Lick Creek became the site of one of that year's biggest news stories. According to later reports, a woman with the last name of Crouch was working on her front porch when meat began falling to the earth. Before the shower was over, more than a half-bushel of fresh meat was flattened across a strip of earth the size of a football field.

In the months that followed this incident, the Kentucky Meat Shower was featured in newspapers and academic journals throughout the United States. Scientists and amateur investigators offered a multitude of speculations about the cause. Early hypotheses ranged from airborne bacteria to meteorites made of meat. A flock of vomiting vultures emerged as one of the most promising explanations for the meatfall. Still, no one knows for certain how a half-bushel of meat fell from the heavens in the late winter of 1876. The very idea of a meat shower seems absurd. When I read the newspaper reports about this event, Mrs Crouch's description of the meat shower sounds a lot like the biblical story of manna falling from the heavens when Moses led the

Israelites through the wilderness—except that what landed in Bath County wasn't sweet bread but raw meat.

So why would anyone today think that this event actually happened?

It's partly because reports related to this event can be traced to multiple witnesses who had little or nothing to gain by making their claims. One former trapper even picked up one of the larger chunks of meat and, after chewing it for a few moments, declared it to be flesh of a bear. Newspaper reports preserve the names not only of Mrs Crouch but also of at least four other witnesses who glimpsed the results of this bizarre bestowal from the sky. One of these individuals was a certain Mr Harrison Gill whose truthfulness and integrity were—according to *The New York Times*—'unquestionable'. And so, despite the sheer absurdity of the Kentucky Meat Shower, firsthand testimonies and secondary reports have convinced those who study such matters that dozens of fragments of raw meat did indeed fall to the earth in 1876. And what does such an odd and obscure historical event have to do with why someone might choose to trust the Bible? Simply this: *the evidence that drives me to admit the plausibility of the Kentucky Meat Shower isn't all that different from what leads me to be open to believing the New Testament Gospels.*

A crucified prophet who returned to life two thousand years ago is inconsistent with all of my day-by-day experiences of life—but so is the claim that Mrs Crouch saw raw meat fall from a cloudless sky in 1876. And yet, testimonies about the Kentucky Meat Shower were shared in a context where witnesses were present and available to discuss what they had seen, and the testimonies came from people who had little or nothing to gain by fabricating their stories. In much the same way, when I examine the New Testament Gospels as historical documents, it seems that these testimonies originated at a time when eyewitnesses were still available in the contexts where the alleged events occurred.

I'm not suggesting that there are no historical problems or unresolved dilemmas in the Gospels (or in the reports of the Kentucky Meat Shower, for that matter). What I *am* contending is that there are good reasons, grounded in evidence, to believe that the New Testament Gospels have preserved testimonies from trustworthy witnesses. One of the first of these reasons has to do with the locations where the stories originated.

WHERE DID THE STORIES ABOUT JESUS COME FROM?

I don't know precisely *how* the Kentucky Meat Shower happened, but I do know *where* the event occurred. Every account of the event identifies a rural region along the southern edge of Bath County, Kentucky as the location of the mysterious meatfall. In 1876, a journey to Bath County required a long ride on a road that was, according to the

New York Herald, in 'first-class bad condition'.[1] I've hiked this region, and the southern perimeter of Bath County is still one of the most backwoods places you'll find anywhere in the Midwestern United States. And yet, early reports related to the Kentucky Meat Shower preserve minute details about this area that would be nearly impossible to know unless the reports originated with people who were there; the newspaper articles mention obscure spots like Slate Creek, Spencer Pike, and an abandoned army barracks from the War of 1812. None of this proves the Kentucky Meat Shower happened, but it does make it unlikely that the event was fabricated by someone sitting in an office in Louisville or Nashville or New York City. Geographical details in the testimonies about this event render the claims far more believable.

That's even more true when it comes to testimonies that were first spoken nearly two thousand years ago, such as the ones that we read in the New Testament Gospels. Today, if you wanted to write about a location you've never visited,

---

1   'The Carnal Rain: Careful Investigation of the Kentucky Marvel by a Correspondent', in *New York Herald* (March 21, 1876). For other reports related to the event, see 'Flesh Descending in a Shower: An Astounding Phenomenon in Kentucky—Fresh Meat Like Mutton or Venison Falling from a Clear Sky', in *The New York Times* (March 10, 1876); J.W.S. Arnold, 'The Kentucky Meat Shower', in *American Journal of Microscopy and Popular Science* (June 1876), 84; L.D. Kastenbine, 'The Kentucky Meat Shower', in *Louisville Medical News* (May 20, 1876), 254-5.

you might be able to unearth enough information on the Internet to fabricate a credible account of a particular place. Even in the nineteenth century, there might have been enough maps of Kentucky available for someone somewhere else to have produced a believable description of Bath County. In the first century A.D., however, there were no maps or texts that included deep topographical details about Judea and Galilee. Yet the descriptions of these locations in the New Testament Gospels reveal intimate knowledge of these locations. This awareness of the topography of these places is so detailed that it's difficult to avoid the conclusion that the stories of Jesus originated among people who had spent time in those locations.[2]

The Gospels reference not only well-known cities like Jerusalem and Tyre but also obscure villages that were virtually unknown beyond the borders of Galilee and Judea—tiny towns like Aenon and Cana, Bethphage and Bethany. And it's not merely the names of communities that are mentioned. The authors of the Gospels also describe very specific topographical trivia. The author of Mark's Gospel

---

2   Data throughout this section have been drawn primarily from Peter Williams, *Can We Trust the Gospels?* (Wheaton: Crossway, 2018), 51-86, and, Richard Bauckham, *Jesus and the Eyewitnesses*, 2nd edition (Grand Rapids: Eerdmans, 2017), 39-92. See also Tal Ilan, *Lexicon of Jewish Names in Late Antiquity*, part 1 (Tübingen: Mohr Siebeck, 2002); Margaret Williams, 'Palestinian Jewish Personal Names in Acts', in *The Book of Acts in Its First Century Setting*, volume 4, ed. Richard Bauckham (Grand Rapids: Eerdmans, 1995), 79-113.

knew, for example, that it was possible to proceed directly from the Sea of Galilee into the Galilean hill country—a detail that, while accurate, would have been unknown outside this region (Mark 3:7, 13; see also Matt. 14:22-23; 15:29). All four Gospels repeatedly reference the fact that a journey to Jerusalem required going uphill (Matt. 20:17-18; Mark 10:32-33; Luke 2:4, 42; 10:30-31; 18:31; 19:28; John 2:13; 5:1; 7:8-14; 11:55; 12:20). John's Gospel records an even more obscure fact, correctly noting that the trip from Cana to Capernaum was downhill (John 2:12). According to Matthew's and Luke's Gospels, Jesus referred to the little-known village of Chorazin in the same context as Bethsaida and Capernaum (Matt. 11:21-23; Luke 10:13-15). As it turns out, archaeological excavations begun in 1869 and completed in 1926 revealed that Chorazin was on the road to Bethsaida, only two or three miles north of Capernaum. And yet, there is no other known text from this era that references Chorazin or its proximity to Bethsaida and Capernaum.

These are only a tiny sample from hundreds of similar examples that reveal intimate knowledge of the topography of the lands that would later become known as Palestine. No one could know such minutiae without either trekking the terrain or writing down testimonies that had been repeated in detail by witnesses who lived in these locations. Not even Josephus or Philo or Strabo—all of whom did describe first-century sites and cities—provided data with the same level of firsthand detail that's packed into the New Testament Gospels.[3]

The genesis of stories about Jesus in the places where the events happened grows even clearer if you pause to examine the names recorded in the Gospels. Although Jewish communities could be found scattered throughout the Roman Empire, contemporary analyses of ancient texts and tomb inscriptions reveal that the names preferred by Jews in Judea and Galilee were different from the monikers that Jewish parents selected elsewhere. The most common names for Jewish males in Judea and Galilee were Simon, Joseph, Lazarus, Judas, John, and Jesus—and these are the same men's names that are most frequent and familiar in the New Testament Gospels. If the accounts behind the New Testament Gospels had been fabricated in other places, it would have been impossible for anyone to have matched these unique naming patterns. There simply weren't enough Judean or Galilean texts available in other regions for anyone to have landed with such consistency on the actual names used in these locales. Many of the naming patterns

---

3   Even if the author of Mark's Gospel does seem to have been uncertain at times about geographical details in Galilee, this does not negate the author's eyewitness awareness of topography in and around Jerusalem. See Martin Hengel, *Studies in the Gospel of Mark* (London: SCM, 1985), 45-47.

shifted after the Romans destroyed the Jewish temple in 70 A.D.; the timing of this change places the rise of the stories of Jesus not only in the places where the alleged events occurred but also in an era that was well within the lifetimes of eyewitnesses.

What these patterns suggest is that the testimonies in the Gospels originated with people from Judea and Galilee. What's more, the stories were preserved in such a way that names and other details were not lost as the testimonies spread from community to community. This provides a certain plausibility when it comes to the suggestion that the testimonies in the Gospels are traceable to the times and places where the events were said to have happened. The Gospels may have been composed in Ephesus or Antioch or Rome, but those cities could not have been where the stories began. The testimonies that were woven into the Gospels originated among women and men with firsthand knowledge of Judea and Galilee. Most important for our purposes, these stories were repeated with such precision that peripheral details were not lost when the stories were written down, even as the Gospel writers adapted their sources to emphasize particular truths about Jesus.

THE POWER OF WORDS FROM THE ONES WHO WERE THERE

One reason why the Kentucky Meat Shower seems so plausible is because the story clearly originated in the location where the alleged event took place—and the Gospels include similar details that reveal intimate knowledge of the locations where the events happened. Another reason for the plausibility of the Kentucky Meat Shower is that testimonies about the meat shower are traceable to eyewitnesses. Even though Mrs Crouch and her grandson were the only people who saw the meat fall from the sky, people from miles around showed up at the Crouch residence soon after the meat fell. None of these witnesses personally penned a record of what they saw, but a *New York Herald* correspondent interviewed the witnesses soon afterward and compiled a comprehensive account of his conversations. More than a century after the alleged event, it's these testimonies that I find most convincing when it comes to the question of whether the Kentucky Meat Shower really happened. Testimonies that are traceable to eyewitnesses multiply the believability of any historical claim.

That's one of the primary reasons why I find the accounts in the New Testament Gospels to be plausible as well. Much of the content in these texts originated with persons who witnessed the events or with close associates of these witnesses.[4] Two of the New Testament Gospels are

---

4   The early authority of apostolic eyewitnesses is observable, e.g., in Acts 1:21-22 where the capacity to exercise apostolic authority among early followers of Jesus was dependent on having been with Jesus and witnessed the resurrection. The capacity of a close associate of an eyewitness to express apostolic truth may be observed, e.g., in

ascribed to Matthew and John, both of whom were said to have been followers of Jesus (Matt. 4:21; 9:9; 10:2-3). The author of John's Gospel explicitly declared that he personally witnessed the events that he described (John 19:35; 21:24). The author of Luke's Gospel never claimed to have been an eyewitness, but the text does suggest that the Gospel includes testimonies from those who walked and talked with Jesus (Luke 1:2). The Gospel According to Mark never mentions the origins of its content, but records from the early second century A.D. reveal that the author gathered his information from Simon Peter. If these connections are correct, the testimonies that were stitched together to form the New Testament Gospels were traceable to eyewitnesses.

But, of course, anyone can claim that their information comes from eyewitnesses. The question is whether these claims make sense on the basis of the evidence.

When it comes to the claim that eyewitness testimony stands behind the New Testament Gospels, there are significant and challenging questions related to whether or not Matthew, Mark, Luke, and John were capable of composing the texts that carry their names. If these four didn't write the Gospels that bear their names, this doesn't mean that the Gospels are fictional, but it could have

---

Justin Martyr, *Dialogi Tryphone,* 103:8, and, Tertullian of Carthage, *Adversus Marcionem,* 4:2.

significant implications for whether testimonies in the New Testament are plausible.

AUTHORSHIP AND LITERACY IN THE FIRST-CENTURY ROMAN EMPIRE

According to some estimates, fewer than 15 per cent of people in the Roman Empire could read and write.[5] The percentage of persons who possessed the capacity to produce literary texts would have been even lower. According to one biblical scholar:

> Jesus' own followers were mainly lower-class peasants—fishermen and artisans. ... If they did have any kind of facility in Greek, it would have been simply for rough communication at best. ... In the end, it seems unlikely that the uneducated, lower-class, illiterate disciples of Jesus played the decisive role in the literary compositions that have come down through history under their names.[6]

---

5   For a more optimistic perspective, see A.R. Millard, *Reading and Writing in the Time of Jesus* (New York: New York University Press, 2000), 154-85. For a range of other perspectives, see William Harris, *Ancient Literacy* (Cambridge: Harvard University Press, 1991); Teresa Morgan, *Literate Education in the Hellenistic and Roman Worlds* (Cambridge: Cambridge University Press, 1999); Catherine Hezser, *Jewish Literacy in Roman Palestine* (Tübingen: Mohr-Siebeck, 2001).

6   Bart Ehrman, *Jesus, Apocalyptic Prophet of the New Millennium* (New York: Oxford University, 1999), 45.

On this point, this scholar may be correct. Galilean fishermen and artisans would probably have had the capacity to read and perhaps even to produce lists and receipts in Greek. Yet the structure and rhetoric of the Gospels required skills in the Greek language that stand far beyond such rudimentary exercises. In each of the four New Testament Gospels, the content is carefully structured, and the use of Greek is simple yet highly skilled, brimming with assonance, alliterations, and subtle allusions to the Greek translation of the Old Testament.

Near a trade crossroads like Capernaum in a multicultural region such as Galilee, I suspect that some of those who first followed Jesus did possess significant skills in the Greek language. And so, my perspective on the disciples' capacity to read and write in Greek is a bit more positive. Yet it's also conceivable that the skeptics are right and none of those who first followed Jesus possessed the necessary skills to pen a biography independently. Matthew was a gatherer of taxes and tolls who—according to the Gospel that bears his name—abandoned his collection booth to follow Jesus (Matt. 9:9; 10:3). Given the negative view of tax gatherers in Matthew's context, it's unlikely that anyone fabricated this origin story. An individual in this role might have enjoyed basic literary capacities and even carried a wax-coated tablet on which to take notes. Still, Matthew seems to have been a lower-level toll collector, and there is no guarantee that such an individual would have possessed the literary skills necessary to produce the simple eloquence and intricate organization of Matthew's Gospel.

It's far from certain whether a fisherman such as the apostle John would have been capable of composing a biography of Jesus. Too little is known about Mark to be confident about what literary training he might have had. Luke was not among the first followers of Jesus, but he seems more likely than any of the others to have had the capacity to formulate a literary text. Luke was a physician, according to a comment in one of the letters in the New Testament (Colossians 4:14). Some physicians in the ancient world may have been trained in ways that would have enabled them to produce complex compositions, but many physicians were poorly equipped when it came to literacy.[7]

So does this mean that the New Testament Gospels were falsely ascribed to Matthew, Mark, Luke, and John? Not necessarily—but these questions do call us to take a closer look at the nature of authorship in the first century. What contemporary readers sometimes misunderstand is the multifaceted nature of authorship in the Greco-Roman world. In the first place, literary skills in the era of the Roman

---

7   For a range of examples related to the literary capacities and literacy of physicians, see Janet Huskinson, *Experiencing Rome* (London: Routledge, 2000), 179-80; Millard, *Reading and Writing in the Time of Jesus*, 183; Vivian Nutton, *Ancient Medicine* (New York: Routledge, 2004), 69, 263-4.

Empire weren't necessarily linked to social status. Someone in the upper echelons of Roman society may have lacked the capacity to write, but this same individual might own a slave who could read fine literature, compose letters, and even produce literary texts. In the contexts in which the Gospels were written, it would have been perfectly conceivable for a professional secretary or scribe to compose a literary text in the name of the source who provided the content. Before being identified as the author, this source would have reviewed and approved the secretary's composition, which would then have circulated under the source's name. Biblical scholar Armin Baum has demonstrated that such a process was recognized as legitimate and appropriate as long as the wording or the content of a particular text could be traced back to the person in whose name the text was published.[8] Secretaries may have crafted some of the epistles in the New Testament in precisely this way in partnership with the apostolic authors (see Rom. 16:22; 1 Pet. 5:12). And so—even if the skeptics are correct in their estimation of the literary capacities of Matthew, Mark, Luke, and John—that doesn't mean these individuals were incapable of authoring the biographies that bear their names. Simply because someone lacked the personal capacity to compose a complex literary text in the first century A.D. doesn't

---

8   Armin Baum, 'Content and Form', *Journal of Biblical Literature* 136 (2017), 384-8.

mean this individual couldn't have been the author of such a composition.

WHAT IF YOU BOUGHT THIS BOOK AND MY NAME WAS MISSING?

But how is it possible to determine who was responsible for the content in the New Testament Gospels?

Well, let's suppose for a moment that this book—the one you're holding right now—failed to include my name anywhere in the book. How would you determine who was the source behind the words that you're reading? One option would be to comb the contents of this book carefully. If you undertook this internal survey of the contents, you would deduce that the author of this book is a scholar of Scripture with a research doctorate who lives with his wife and daughters in the city of Louisville. That would narrow the possibilities down to a relatively small handful of people. From that point, you might be able to glean enough information about my writing style, my personal eccentricities, and my obsession with the Kentucky Meat Shower to determine that the author of this book is me. Another approach would be to look for external information about this book. If that's the path you chose, you could try to find reviews of the book, catalogs that list the book, perhaps even emails between the publisher and me.

In the end, you would be looking for *what others have said about the book* and *what the book says about itself.* That's similar to what we can look for when it comes to the question of who wrote the New Testament Gospels. It's a little more difficult when it comes to the Gospels than it would be for this particular book, due to the fact that the Gospels were written nearly two thousand years ago with very few internal hints about authorship. And yet, there are clues—both inside and outside the Gospels—that reveal much about the origins of these texts.

WHAT OTHERS HAVE SAID ABOUT THE NEW TESTAMENT GOSPELS

The earliest surviving reference to the origins of the Gospels can be found in the writings of Papias of Hierapolis. Papias was a pastor who served a church in western Asia Minor in the late first and early second centuries. Here, near a popular crossroads, he collected oral histories about Jesus and the Gospels from Christians who were journeying across the region known today as Turkey. Here's what Papias picked up from these conversations about the first two Gospels:

> Matthew, in the Hebrew dialect, placed sayings in orderly arrangement, and each one translated them as he was able. ... Mark, who became Peter's translator, wrote accurately as much as he remembered—though not in ordered form—of the Lord's sayings and doings. For he neither heard the Lord nor followed after him

but later—as I said—he followed after Peter, who was giving his teachings in short anecdotes. ... Mark had one purpose—to omit nothing of what he had heard and to present no false testimony.[9]

Papias admitted that Mark never met Jesus, but he pointed out that Mark's information came to him from Simon Peter, a man who knew Jesus well. He also recognized that Matthew's initial work was done 'in the Hebrew dialect'— probably a reference to the Aramaic language, which shares the same alphabet as Hebrew—and that those reading the text translated Matthew's words to the best of their ability. In both cases, it's clear that these Gospels were composed from testimonies that originated among eyewitnesses.[10]

---

9   Eusebius of Caesarea, *Historia Ecclesiastica,* 5:8:2-4. The Gospel According to Matthew that survives in Greek includes word-plays and other rhetorical features that only work in Greek, suggesting that this text is not a translation from Aramaic. It is not inconceivable that Matthew authored a Gospel in Aramaic and that the Greek Gospel According to Matthew is an independent literary production developed from Matthew's Gospel in Aramaic. The Jewish historian Josephus initially composed his history of the Jewish war in Aramaic; the Greek composition is an independent literary composition that involved the work of secretaries. Like the Gospel According to Matthew, the Aramaic version of the history of the Jewish war does not survive, and the Greek version shows no signs of being a translation from its Aramaic predecessor. See Josephus, *Contra Apionem,* 1:50.

10   The historian Eusebius seems also to have preserved a report from a Papias regarding the Gospels According to Luke and John. See Charles Hill, 'What Papias Said about John (and Luke)', in *Journal of Theological Studies* 49 (1998), 582-629.

Not long after Papias wrote these words, someone seems to have passed on similar information to a student of Polycarp, another church leader in Asia Minor. This student's name was Irenaeus, and he later served as a pastor in the Aquitaine region of France. That's where Irenaeus was living when he wrote this summary of the origins of the four Gospels in the late second century A.D.:

> Matthew composed his Gospel among the Hebrews in their language, while Peter and Paul were preaching the Gospel in Rome and building up the church there. After their exodus, Peter's follower and translator Mark handed down to us Peter's proclamation in written form. Luke, Paul's companion, wrote in a book the Gospel proclaimed by Paul. Finally, John—the Lord's own follower, the one who leaned against his chest—composed the Gospel while living in Ephesus.

Another record from around the same time corroborates what Irenaeus of Lyon had to say about the Gospels. According to a text that seems to have originated in the city of Rome:

> the third book of the Gospel is 'according to Luke.' After the ascension of the Messiah, Paul took Luke with him. ... Luke the physician composed this Gospel in his own name, just as it has been told. He himself had not seen the Lord in the flesh; still, he personally investigated certain events, and he begins to relate his

account from John's birth. The fourth of the Gospels is
the one 'according to John,' one of the disciples.

In the opening decade of the third century, a North African
writer named Tertullian similarly identified the four New
Testament Gospels as the works of Matthew, Mark, Luke,
and John: 'John and Matthew, of the apostles, first instill
faith into us while the apostolic writers Luke and Mark
renew it afterwards.'[11]

Throughout the century that followed the writing of the
New Testament Gospels, every surviving document that
discusses the origins of these texts traces them back to the
same four individuals. These reports originated in locations
that were separated by hundreds of miles. Yet they agree in
particular details that are unlikely to have been fabricated,
such as the initial composition of Matthew's Gospel in a
dialect that used Hebrew letters and the admission that
neither Luke nor Mark had personally followed Jesus. If
no one knew who wrote the Gospels when this quartet of
texts began to circulate, it is difficult to explain how these
compositions became so quickly and consistently connected
to Matthew, Mark, Luke, and John across such variegated

---

11 Quotations from primary source materials are translated from
    Irenaeus of Lyon, *Adversus Haereses,* 3:1:1-2; 'The Muratorian
    Canon': http://www.earlychristianwritings.com; Tertullian of
    Carthage, *Adversus Marcionem,* 4:2. For Irenaeus as a disciple of
    Polycarp, see Eusebius of Caesarea, *Historia Ecclesiastica,* 5:20:4-8.

geographical contexts. Much like the initial reports about the Kentucky Meat Shower, the stories in these four ancient compositions seem to have originated among eyewitnesses of the original events, and accounts of the events can be traced back to known and named witnesses.

WHAT THE GOSPEL MANUSCRIPTS SAY ABOUT THEMSELVES

But to whom were the Gospels ascribed during the first few decades after they were written? Were these texts already titled and recognized as the work of Matthew, Mark, Luke, and John when they first began to circulate? Or did those connections come later?

Some scholars have suggested that the actual authors of the Gospels were anonymous first-century Christians who never met Jesus. Some of these same scholars suggest that the names of Matthew, Mark, Luke, and John were never linked to the texts until sometime in the mid-second century. According to this line of thinking, that's when church leaders fabricated connections between the four Gospels and well-known first-century Christians for the purpose of making the Gospels seem more authoritative. Here's how one scholar summarizes this perspective:

> When ... Christians recognized the need for *apostolic* authorities, they attributed these books to apostles (Matthew and John) and close companions of apostles

> (Mark, the secretary of Peter; and Luke the traveling companion of Paul). ... Scholars continue to call these books Matthew, Mark, Luke, and John as a matter of convenience; they have to be called *something*, and it doesn't make much sense to call them George, Jim, Fred, and Sam.[12]

So what was the earliest ascription for each of these texts? Are the names Matthew, Mark, Luke, and John nothing more than 'a matter of convenience', disconnected from any historical reality? Or was there something more going on in the naming of these texts than a gathering of church leaders that fabricated titles to bolster the perceived authority of their preferred Gospels?

There's no way to settle this question by examining the original manuscripts. Those documents decayed into dust more than a millennium ago. Fragments of the Gospels may survive from the second century, but none of these early fragments include the portions of the pages where titles would have been recorded. The earliest copies of the Gospels that survive sufficiently intact for the titles to have been preserved were probably produced in the third century A.D.; these papyrus portions of the Gospels include the texts known as P4 (Suppl. Greek 1120 ii 3), P66 (Papyrus Bodmer II), and P75 (Papyrus Bodmer XIV-XV). Without

---

12 Ehrman, *Jesus, Apocalyptic Prophet of the New Millennium*, 44-6; Bart Ehrman, *Lost Christianities* (New York: Oxford University Press, 2003), 235.

exception, these copies and the myriads of intact copies that come after them do include titles that ascribe the Gospels to Matthew, Mark, Luke, and John.

In favor of the possibility that the authors' names were added later is the fact that there may have been a point at which the *form* of the Gospel titles was standardized. The titles of all four Gospels are phrased in a similar and somewhat unique way: the Gospel 'according to' the author. This distinct usage of 'according to' in each Gospel title could mean that early Christians standardized these titles at some point. Alternatively, it might also mean that the author of the earliest Gospel used this form to title his text, and the copyists of later Gospels simply followed a pattern that was familiar to them and to their readers.

If the titles of the Gospels were in fact standardized midway through the second century, it's conceivable that fictitious connections to particular authors were forged at that time as well—but there's another possibility that I find far more plausible. What seems more likely is that the *authors* of the Gospels were well-known from the time that each text first began to circulate, even if the *form* of the titles was standardized later. Here are a couple of reasons why it seems that the authors of the Gospels were well known from the earliest stages:

*1. IF CONNECTIONS TO CERTAIN FIRST-CENTURY PERSON-
ALITIES HAD BEEN FABRICATED IN THE SECOND CENTURY,
IT'S UNLIKELY THAT CHRISTIANS WOULD HAVE SELECTED
THESE FOUR NAMES:*

The most significant reason why it seems unlikely that connections to Matthew, Mark, Luke, and John were fabricated at a later time is the names themselves. If second-century Christians had forged links to four prominent first-century personalities, why would these four individuals have been the ones they selected? Ascribing a Gospel to the apostle John makes sense—but, if church leaders were trying to bolster the perceived authority of these texts, it would have made far more sense to ascribe a Gospel to Peter, James, or Paul than to have assigned Gospels to Matthew, Mark, and Luke. That's particularly true when it comes to the Gospel that's ascribed to Luke. Yes, Luke was one of Paul's traveling partners—but why would anyone have chosen Luke's name in an attempt to claim Paul's authority for this Gospel?[13] Naming the text 'Gospel According to Paul' or even 'Gospel According to Timothy' or 'Gospel According to Titus' would have been a far shrewder choice than assigning the text to

---

13 Early Christians recognized that Luke traveled with Paul. The salutation and style of Luke's Gospel and the Acts of the Apostles are very similar, and the author of the book of Acts implicitly identifies himself as a traveling companion of Paul by shifting to the first-person plural at certain points in Acts (16:10-17; 20:5-15; 21:1-18; 27:1-37; 28:1-16).

Luke, an obscure character who's mentioned only three times in the entire Bible by name (Col. 4:14; 2 Tim. 4:11; Philem. 1:24). Timothy and Titus were better known, and their names would have carried significantly more weight (Acts 15:40–18:5; 2 Cor. 1:1, 19; 8:23; Gal. 2:1-3; Phil. 1:1; Col. 1:1; 1 Thess. 1:1; 2 Thess. 1:1; Philem. 1:1). In the end, Luke's obscurity is one of the strongest evidences for the authenticity of this ascription of a Gospel to him. There is no reason why this text should be ascribed to Luke unless early Christians knew that Luke was the source behind this Gospel.

2. *If connections to certain first-century personalities had been fabricated in the second century, later manuscripts would probably have ascribed the same Gospel to different authors:*

In the opening decade of the second century A.D., Papias already knew at least two of the New Testament Gospels, revealing that these Gospels had already circulated at least as far as the western regions of Asia Minor. The writings of Irenaeus, Tertullian, and other church leaders reveal that, before the end of the second century, all four Gospels were scattered across most of the Roman Empire, from Italia and Gaul to Asia Minor and even into Egypt and North Africa.[14] Now, let's consider for a moment what might have happened if no

---

14   John Barton, *A History of the Bible* (New York: Viking, 2019), 202.

one ascribed the Gospels to Matthew, Mark, Luke, and John until midway through the second century when these connections were allegedly fabricated. If the Gospels had already circulated until the mid-second century with no consensus about who had produced them, different people in different places would have developed different traditions and titles for each Gospel. As a result, when titles began to be added in different locations, conflicting authors would likely have been ascribed to the same Gospels in early manuscripts and in the writings of second-century church leaders. And yet, that's not even close to what we find in the actual texts and manuscripts. *Every Gospel manuscript that survives sufficiently intact to include a title has a title, and that title assigns the text to the same author to which that Gospel is ascribed in Bibles today.* There is no wide variety of different titles in early manuscripts of the Gospels.[15] There are a handful of spelling variants and a few variations in the forms of the titles, but there is no variation in the ascribed authors. This unanimity is almost impossible to explain unless early Christian congregations had already connected the Gospels to Matthew, Mark, Luke, or John prior to the mid-second century.

15　This claim may be found in Ehrman, *Jesus, Apocalyptic Prophet of the New Millennium*, 248-9; see also pages 42-3. For a survey of titles in the earliest manuscripts, see Simon Gathercole, 'The Titles of the Gospels in the Earliest New Testament Manuscripts', in *Zeitschrift für die Neutestamentliche Wissenschaft und die Kunde der älteren Kirche* 104 (2013), 33-76.

The communities that first received the New Testament Gospels knew the sources behind these four texts, and the sources they knew were Matthew, Mark, Luke, and John. Whether or not the New Testament Gospels tell the truth, the strongest evidence suggests that these texts originated with persons who were in a position to know what Jesus said and did. Even if Matthew, Mark, Luke, and John never personally placed pens on paper to compose the texts that bear their names, they provided the content that was crafted into the Gospels we know today. Furthermore, when the four Gospels were first issued in the second half of the first century, many eyewitnesses would still have been present and accessible in the churches, and these congregations were communities in constant communication with one another. In such a context, it's highly unlikely that these biographies of Jesus would have circulated widely if they conflicted with the spoken reports of eyewitnesses at a time when these individuals were still alive.

WHO AUTHORED THE GOSPELS?

Much like newspaper reports that make the Kentucky Meat Shower so plausible, the stories in the Gospels originated in the regions where the alleged events took place, and their claims can be traced to eyewitnesses. The testimony in John's Gospel came from an early follower of Jesus named John. Mark's Gospel originated with someone who had translated stories shared by Simon Peter. The Gospels According to Matthew and Luke adapted and expanded content from Mark's Gospel. In Matthew's Gospel, these expansions included the reminiscences of a follower of Jesus. Luke never walked with Jesus, but the content that he combined with Mark's Gospel included testimonies from women and men who had encountered Jesus (Luke 1:2). If authorship is defined in the same way that first-century hearers understood authorship, there are good reasons to be confident that Matthew, Mark, Luke, and John were the authors of the New Testament Gospels. This confidence is grounded in external evidence from other texts as well as internal evidence from early New Testament manuscripts.

In a survey as brief as this one, there's not sufficient space to summarize every fact and artifact that supports what I'm suggesting; in this chapter in particular, I've left out far more evidence than I've left in. My hope has been simply to provide you with enough evidence to whet your intellectual appetite and to open a door for you to explore these issues further. In the end, you may find the evidence to be compelling, or you may conclude that it's still not enough. Either way, what should be clear is that anyone who trumpets the accusation that there is a 'total absence of supporting evidence' for trust in what the Gospels say is misrepresenting reality.[16] What

---

16   Dawkins, *The Selfish Gene*, 330.

Christians believe may be right or it may be wrong, but there are substantive historical reasons to receive the New Testament Gospels as biographies grounded in trustworthy testimony.

I don't pretend that the Gospels are easy to believe. They aren't. If the content in the Gospels had been limited to the sermons Jesus preached and the parables he told, his teachings would still have been difficult to follow, but the claims would be far easier to swallow. This quartet of biographies is filled with far more, however, than the fiery words of an apocalyptic prophet. From start to finish, the Gospel texts overflow with claims that refuse to conform to the ideological framework of a secular world. The story of Jesus is framed by a virgin conception at the beginning and a resurrection at the end, with healings and visions entwined with voices from heaven in between. The unavoidable claim of the Gospels is that these events happened in the context of human history. There is no honest way to geld or tame these texts so that they fit easily within a modern mindset. The Gospels are weird and wild, and they defy domestication. And yet, even after decades of examining the form and the content of these documents, I find myself still convinced by the evidence that they are true.

CAN A MIRACULOUS CLAIM EVER BE PLAUSIBLE?

Some scholars have responded to the strangeness of miracles by arguing that no miraculous event can ever be considered historically probable or plausible, regardless of the evidence. A miracle such as resurrection would be—according to one proponent of this perspective—:

> a violation of what naturally happens, every day, time after time, millions of times a year. ... By the very nature of the canons of historical research, we can't claim historically that a miracle probably happened. By definition, it probably didn't, and history can only establish what probably did.[17]

According to this line of reasoning, the 'canons of historical research' rule out any likelihood of miracles, because history can only acknowledge what is probable and miracles are always improbable.

The first problem with this logic is that these supposed 'canons of historical research' are a recent invention, and not every historian agrees that these are the rules by which

---

17 Bart Ehrman, 'Is There Historical Evidence for the Resurrection of Jesus?' (debate with William Lane Craig, March 28, 2006). Whether intentionally or unintentionally, Ehrman assumes here Ernst Troeltsch's principle of analogy. According to Troeltsch's principle of analogy, historians' understanding of the past must be analogically grounded in their experience of the present. See Ernst Troeltsch's 1898 essay 'Historical and Dogmatic Method in Theology', reprinted in *Religion in History*, translated by J.L. Adams and W.F. Bense (Minneapolis: Fortress, 1991), 11-32.

historical research must be governed. A second and more pressing problem is that—if the standard for gauging historical probability is 'what naturally happens, every day, time after time'—the Kentucky Meat Shower should not be considered historical. For that matter, neither should dozens of other improbable events that have no analogy in common human experience, including Hannibal's advance over the Alps on elephants in the third century B.C. and the twelfth-century arrival of two green-skinned children in the English village of Woolpit.[18] Neither of these events was miraculous in the sense that it required supernatural intervention—but both of these events and a multitude of other historical happenings are highly improbable and probably unrepeatable. Each one was 'a violation of what naturally happens, every day, time after time' in common human experience. And yet, they're widely recognized as actual happenings.

The frequency of an event in ordinary human experience is not what determines its probability in history. What makes improbable events plausible is not *frequency* but *evidence*, and the evidences that support the reality of such events don't have to be extraordinary. Whether an event is rare or commonplace, the historicity of the event must be assessed

---

18 Paul Harris, 'The Green Children of Woolpit', in *Fortean Studies: 4* (London: John Brown, 1998), 81-95; John Prevas, *Hannibal Crosses the Alps* (Boston: Da Capo, 2001).

on the basis of ordinary evidences like memories and texts and physical artifacts, regardless of whether the alleged cause is natural, supernatural, or somewhere between. If someone makes a claim that has no natural explanation, it makes sense to examine the evidence with a bit of skepticism. And yet, there is a vast difference between such healthy skepticism and a methodological presupposition that removes any possibilities that might defy natural explanation from potential consideration on the basis of supposed 'canons of historical research'.

If the resurrection of Jesus did indeed happen in history, this return from death stands as a rare reversal of every typical pattern of human life and death; Christians have never suggested otherwise. I would suggest, however, that the resurrection of Jesus is implausible if and only if you have already decided that supernatural intervention in history is always the least probable possibility. And, if you've already presupposed that supernatural possibilities belong in a special category of improbability separate from other improbable happenings, it's worth considering the possibility that this presupposition may have predetermined your conclusions prior to any open-minded examination of the evidence.

THE FORK IN THE ROAD

Our journey has now brought us to an unavoidable point of potential separation. Up to this point, I have approached the Gospels not as holy Scripture but simply as ancient compositions that make particular historical claims. I have not argued that the texts are perfect, only that they include trustworthy testimony that's traceable to eyewitnesses in the locations where the alleged events occurred. The evidence that I've presented suggests that these texts are biographies constructed from historically-reliable testimonies.

In the end, I do find the claims in the Gospels to be both plausible and probable, particularly when it comes to the claim that the corpse of a crucified Jew made the ultimate comeback two thousand years ago. Multiple independent witnesses testify together to the truth of this claim. The resurrection of Jesus appears not only in the four Gospels but also in an early oral history recorded by Paul (Matt. 27:62–28:1; Mark 8:31; 9:31; 10:34; 16:1-2; Luke 24:1-49; John 19:38–20:2; 1 Cor. 15:3-7). The details differ, but all of these disparate accounts agree that Jesus died and then returned to life three days later. So does an independent but secondhand report composed in the second century and preserved in a later document known as the Akhmim Fragment.[19] All but one of these reports also include incidental details such as the

---

19 For more on the Akhmim Fragment (P. Cair. 10759), see Paul Foster, *The Gospel of Peter* (Brill: Leiden, 2010).

claim that Mary Magdalene was the first witness—a detail that was unlikely to have been fabricated in a first-century context where there was systemic bias against testimony from women. If the Jews of the first century A.D. expected any resurrection at all, it would have been a resurrection of all the righteous at the end of time. They knew that death was typically a one-way street, and they were fully aware of alternative explanations such as post-mortem dreams and hallucinations. And still, somehow, the men and women who first followed Jesus concluded that what they saw three days after Jesus died required the physical resuscitation of a previously deceased person, and they shared the news of this resurrection from one end of the Roman Empire to the other.

What's more, encounters with the resurrected Jesus reshaped the lives of certain witnesses in such a way that they eventually chose death over any denial of what they proclaimed about Jesus. At the very least, Simon Peter, James the son of Zebedee, and James the brother of Jesus died for what they declared about Jesus.[20] Of course, millions of people throughout history have died for lies that they believed were true—but people do not typically give

---

20 Sean Joslin McDowell, 'A Historical Evaluation of the Evidence for the Deaths of the Apostles as Martyrs for their Faith' (Ph.D. dissertation, The Southern Baptist Theological Seminary, 2014), 103-54, 194-258, 424-9.

their lives for a lie if they're in a position to know that it's a lie. If anyone might have been in a position to know that the claims of resurrection were fabrications, one or more of these three men would have known. And yet, all three of them went to their deaths still declaring that Jesus had been raised from the dead. Either Peter and the two Jameses were convinced that Jesus was raised and they were mistaken, or they were convinced and they were correct. Based on the evidence, it seems more likely to me that they were right than that they were wrong.

I am fully aware that I might be in error about the Gospels and about the resurrection. There is no mathematical or scientific proof for these claims—but, once again, that's true of any event in history. When doing history, what we are seeking is not proof but plausibility and probability, and such probability is attained only by examining the possibilities and asking how well each possibility explains the claims being made.[21] Belief in any past event is an act of faith; the crucial question has to do with whether this faith is internally coherent and grounded in evidence. In the end, the stories in the Gospels seem to me to make better sense of the possibilities than any of the alternatives. I have found no purely natural explanation that can plausibly account for all the evidence surrounding the events that led early Christians

---

21 John Henry Newman, *An Essay in Aid of a Grammar of Assent* (repr. ed., Westminster: Christian Classics, 1973), 288.

to make the claims that they made. Only the resurrection of Jesus provides a necessary and sufficient explanation for the faith of the first followers of Jesus.[22]

Historical evidence for the resurrection was one of the means that moved me from a flimsy faith followed by skepticism to the faith by which I live today. This faith arose within me at a time in my life when I had little to gain by believing it and little to lose by denying it. Three decades after those weeks in the library, my trust in Jesus and in the Bible is still grounded in a confidence that the Gospels—even when read simply as historical documents—provide the most plausible reconstruction of what happened, especially when it comes to their reports about the resurrection of Jesus.

And that's what brings us to this point of separation.

If you're open to the possibility that the Gospels tell the truth and that Jesus was raised from the dead, the rest of this book will help you to see how a reasonable person might end up trusting the rest of the Bible. If you've already decided that no supernatural explanation can ever be admissible as history, what I say in the chapters that follow this one will not convince you that the Bible is trustworthy. But— if you've already presumed that events can be considered

---

22 For the implications of necessary and sufficient conditions related to views of the resurrection, see N.T. Wright, *The Resurrection of the Son of God* (Minneapolis: Fortress, 2003), chapter 18.

historical only if they have a natural explanation—I would ask you to consider whether you may have reached this verdict not on the basis of the evidence but on the basis of your presuppositions. Either way, I hope that you'll remain with me for the rest of this journey. But we have reached a point where the path for those who reject the plausibility of the resurrection diverges unavoidably from the path that I have marked out for the remainder of this book.

RECOMMENDED RESOURCES

Bauckham, Richard. *Jesus and the Eyewitnesses.* 2nd edition. (Grand Rapids: Eerdmans, 2017).

Boyd, Gregory, and Paul Eddy. *The Jesus Legend.* (Grand Rapids: Baker, 2007).

Licona, Michael. *The Resurrection of Jesus.* (Downers Grove: InterVarsity, 2011).

Williams, Peter. *Can We Trust the Gospels?* (Wheaton: Crossway, 2018).

Wright, N.T. *The Resurrection of the Son of God.* (Minneapolis: Fortress, 2003).

4

Which Books Belong in the Bible?

Since the Bible is typically printed as a single book, it's tempting to treat the Bible as if it's a single text penned by a single author in a single genre. Yet the Bible isn't a single book at all; the Bible includes dozens of books composed in a variety of genres over the span of more than a millennium by God-only-knows how many different authors. The good book isn't actually a book; it's a library.

The New Testament Gospels are central documents in this library, but this quartet of biographies never stands alone. The Gospels were composed in continuity with the Old Testament, and they cannot be unhitched from the earlier stories of Abraham and Isaac and Israel. Before the Gospels were even completed, first-century church leaders like James and John and Paul were already fleshing out the implications of Jesus's life by sending letters to early communities of Christians. These epistles are included in the New Testament alongside the Gospels and Acts. Together, this collection of texts forms a library with two primary sections, the Old Testament and the New Testament.

Christians throughout the ages have regarded this library of texts as uniquely authoritative and true. Whether or not you agree that the Bible is true, the fact that the Bible draws together such a multifaceted kaleidoscope of texts should trigger at least a few questions in your mind: Who decided which texts belong in this library? Why did they choose the books they chose? And who's to say they made the right decision? The question of whether the Bible should be trusted can't be answered without considering the question of how these particular books ended up together in the first place. Trusting the Bible means trusting not only the books themselves but also the processes by which the books were gathered together.

Unfortunately, many people—including a surprising number of Christians who say they believe the Bible— have completely incorrect ideas about how this library was assembled in the first place. One common solution to this enigma is to declare that, at some point in the first few centuries of Christianity, church leaders gathered together and God told them which books belonged in the Bible. No such gathering ever happened, but the myth is popular nonetheless. I was recently reminded how many Christians believe this myth when I made the mistake of reading a review of one of my own books.

How can you talk about the invention of the light bulb and not mention Elvis Presley?

I rarely read reviews of anything I write, but I made an exception when a colleague sent me a link to an online review of one of my books. Someone was apparently disappointed with a history of the Bible that I had produced. The reviewer slapped the book with a two-star rating on a five-star scale and entitled her review 'Not Much Historical Information.'

What caught my attention in the review wasn't the fact that this individual disliked what I wrote. A lot of people can't stand certain books that I've written, including my own children and nearly everyone in the churches in which I grew up. Some days, when I'm reviewing what I've written, I completely agree with their assessments. What interested me was what this reviewer thought I'd failed to cover between the covers of this particular book.

'My Bible study class wanted to learn more about how the Bible came to be compiled,' she wrote. 'We ordered this in hopes to gain more information on the Council of Nicaea—which books were and were not chosen and why.' At this point, the reviewer—who was, I'm certain, well-intended and sincere in her disappointment—launched into a critique of the book's failure to describe in detail how the leaders of the Church chose the books of the Bible at the Council of Nicaea. At the culmination of her review, she declared in apparent despair, 'One of my Bible study members remarked, "How can he talk about how the Bible came to be and not mention the Council of Nicaea?" My point exactly.'

The Council of Nicaea was a gathering of church leaders that took place in the year 325 A.D., about eighty miles south of the metropolis known today as Istanbul, Turkey. If this council had made any decisions whatsoever about which texts ended up in the Bible, the reviewer's concerns would have made perfect sense. The problem is, however, that the Council of Nicaea had nothing to do with any aspect of how the Bible was brought together. Asking 'How can he talk about how the Bible came to be and not mention the Council of Nicaea?' is like asking, 'How can you talk about the invention of the electric light bulb and not mention Elvis Presley?' The Council of Nicaea had every bit as much to do with the formation of the Bible as Elvis had to do with the creation of the electric light bulb. Elvis may have benefited from the light bulb, but he had nothing to do with its invention.

The church leaders who made the journey to Nicaea in the fourth century traveled there to discuss what the first-century apostles had taught about the nature of Jesus. Over the space of three months, the council composed a creed and discussed at least twenty issues, including whether pastors could be married and whether or not the apostles had thought Jesus was fully divine (their answer was 'yes' to both of these questions). And yet, as far as anyone can tell from the historical evidence, nothing related to the books of the Bible was discussed, decided, or declared at the Council of Nicaea.

HOW A MEDIEVAL MYTH MADE ITS WAY INTO THE MODERN MIND

Why, then, are so many people convinced that the Council of Nicaea had something to do with which books ended up in the Bible?

It seems that this mistruth may be traceable to a myth that emerged in the Middle Ages.

According to an anonymous document from the ninth century A.D., church leaders at the Council of Nicaea piled all the books that were candidates for inclusion in the Bible on a communion table and prayed. As they prayed, all the spurious texts slipped through the table and crashed to the floor. The Bible was formed from the books that stayed on top of the table.[1] If this really happened, it would greatly

---

1   For the tale of the determination of the canon at the Council of Nicaea, see *The Synodicon Vetus,* in *Corpus Fontium Historiae Byzantinae,* volume 15 (Washington, D.C.: Dumbarton Oaks, 1979). In Jerome's prologue to his Latin translation of the book of Judith, Jerome did state that he was grudgingly translating this apocryphal text 'because this book was considered by the Nicene Council to have been counted among the number of the sacred Scriptures.' However, Jerome did not state that the canonicity of the book was discussed at the Council of Nicaea; his point seems to

simplify the question of how certain books ended up in the Bible. (Also, if such a trial by ordeal really worked, I would be tempted to try it whenever two or more of my children give me contradictory reports about who did what. Each time my children's stories conflicted with one another, I would simply seat the four of them in a row on the coffee table, pray until the less-truthful children hit the floor, and then give cookies to everyone who stayed on top of the table.)

Unfortunately for the question of which texts belong in the Bible (as well as for my capacity to discern which ones of my children are telling the truth), there is no reliable evidence that any such event ever took place at Nicaea or anywhere else. This seems like the sort of bizarre occurrence that people would talk about after the council was over, yet no one who attended the Council of Nicaea ever mentioned any event of this sort. The earliest description of this alleged selection of books shows up in a single document copied more than six centuries after the final session of the council. As such, no modern scholar has ever taken seriously this account of the formation of the Bible. Simply put, the table of contents in your Bible was not formed from the content that stayed on top of the table at the Council of Nicaea.

An eighteenth-century philosopher named Voltaire popularized the myth of this literary ordeal when he

---

have been that the participants in the Council utilized the book of Judith as Scripture.

satirized it in his philosophical dictionary. From that point forward, links between the Council of Nicaea and which books ended up in the Bible have continued to pop up in popular descriptions of the formation of the Bible. In 2005, Dan Brown connected the Council of Nicaea to the creation of the Bible in his bestselling novel *The Da Vinci Code,* but Brown also added a twist that he had picked up from some twentieth-century conspiracy theories. According to *The Da Vinci Code,* it was not the leaders of the Church but Constantine the emperor who collated and edited the books of the Bible at the Council of Nicaea.[2] And so, a medieval myth wormed its way into the modern imagination through a satirical philosopher, a handful of conspiracy theorists, and a bestselling novelist.

A Jesus-shaped Bible

So—if the Bible didn't take shape at the Council of Nicaea— how and when was this library gathered together? And what was the rationale for why some books ended up in the Bible and others didn't? Regardless of whether you see the Bible as God's perfect Word or as a substandard mingling of patriarchal oppression and premodern fairy tales, it isn't helpful to refuse to reckon with the messy complexities of how these books came together. And so, what I want to do

---

2   Dan Brown, *The Da Vinci Code* (New York: Doubleday, 2003), 231-3.

in this chapter is simply to sketch out the processes by which the Bible evolved into the book that we know today.

Some parts of the process that brought us the Bible were sloppier than many Christians would like to admit. And yet, in the end, I find myself convinced that sixty-six texts rightly and reasonably belong in the Bible—thirty-nine books in the Old Testament and twenty-seven in the New Testament. My rationale for recognizing these books as the right books shouldn't surprise you (unless, of course, you skipped the first three chapters of this book, in which case you deserve to be surprised). What I believe about the books of the Bible is grounded in the resurrection of Jesus and the witness of the New Testament Gospels—texts that, whether divinely inspired or not, seem to have been woven together from reliable, eyewitness testimonies about Jesus.

So what's the connection between the resurrection of Jesus and the enigma of which books belong in the Bible?

If Jesus was raised from the dead, there is a sense in which Jesus's resurrection vindicated his works and his words. And so, if I embrace the historical reliability of the Gospels, it makes sense for me also to recognize the truthfulness and usefulness of whatever Old Testament texts Jesus regarded as uniquely authoritative.

The resurrection of Jesus is equally significant when it comes to the books in the New Testament. The Christian writings that early believers received as authoritative alongside the Old Testament were texts that could be traced to eyewitnesses or close associates of eyewitnesses of the resurrected Jesus. What marked the twenty-seven books of the New Testament as authoritative was whether they could be traced back to individuals who had been commissioned by the resurrected Jesus.

If you've already decided that Jesus is still dead or that he never existed in the first place, none of the patterns that I point out in these pages will convince you that the Bible is true. At best, what I present in these pages will help you to see how someone with presuppositions that differ from yours might recognize certain texts as uniquely useful and true in shaping their faith. If, however, you're open to the possibility that Jesus may have emerged alive from a tomb two thousand years ago, what you'll see in this chapter is how the resurrection of Jesus shapes the very content of the Bible. To trust in the resurrected Jesus is to trust not only Jesus himself but also the texts he trusted and the writings of the witnesses he commissioned to tell the world about him.

HOW THE RESURRECTION OF JESUS SHAPES THE OLD TESTAMENT

If Jesus said anything close to what the Gospels say he said, Jesus believed the Bible. Of course, Jesus didn't have access to the entire corpus of literature that people identify as the Bible today. Jesus knew only the portions of the Bible that his followers would eventually refer to as 'the Old Testament'—but he clearly recognized this corpus as true, and he saw himself as the fulfillment of all that the Old Testament had to say (Matt. 4:4, 7, 10; 5:17; 21:13; Mark 7:6; 11:17; Luke 4:4, 8, 12, 21; 14:46; John 6:31; 10:34).

If Jesus believed his Bible and if I trust what he taught on the basis of the testimony in the Gospels, it makes sense for me to believe the same texts that he believed. But there is a problem when it comes to the books of the Old Testament: Not everyone who claims to follow Jesus today agrees about which books Jesus and his first followers identified as part of the Old Testament.

DIFFERENT CHURCHES, DIFFERENT OLD TESTAMENTS

Different communities of people who read and believe the Bible use different Old Testaments. Here's what I mean: If you attended Mass in a Roman Catholic congregation this weekend, the Old Testament readings would come from a collection that includes seven books beyond the thirty-nine books in the Old Testament at the Protestant church down the street. A few blocks further down the street at the Jewish synagogue, a reader who probably doesn't believe in the resurrection of Jesus at all will be chanting a Hebrew or Aramaic text from the same Old Testament that the Protestants are studying in translated form. The Orthodox Church across town will be reading an Old Testament that encompasses a total of ten more texts than Jews and Protestants recognize.

All of these disparities spawn a difficult question: If people who claim to be Christians can't be sure about which books belong in the Old Testament, how can anyone reasonably believe what the Old Testament has to say?

Some Christians answer this question by appealing to church tradition or to their conviction that the Holy Spirit mystically enables Christians to recognize which books are divinely inspired. Personally, I don't find either of these answers to be the most helpful responses. What I believe about the Bible is grounded in the words of a man who died and rose again. If he's still dead or if later Christians fabricated his teachings, I have no reason to believe the Bible at all. But it seems more plausible to me that Jesus walked out of the tomb than that he remained dead, and the teachings attributed to Jesus in the Gospels seem more likely to have originated with Jesus than with anyone else. Because I believe that Jesus is alive, I trust what Jesus had to say. And so, when I consider which books belong in the Old Testament, my goal is simply to trust the same Old Testament that Jesus trusted.

Before peeling back the layers of history to determine which books Jesus trusted, however, let's first take a look at how different churches ended up with different Old Testaments in the first place.

ARISTOTLE, ALEXANDER, AND THE GREEK OLD TESTAMENT

In some sense, the pathway that led to differences in the Old Testament began with Alexander the Great. Long before Alexander ever rallied an army into battle from the saddle of Bucephalus the warhorse, Alexander was the pupil of a philosopher named Aristotle. Aristotle was convinced that Greek language and culture represented humanity's highest achievement, and his passion for Greek culture seems to have shaped young Alexander's vision for his empire.

When Alexander undertook the military campaigns that would win him a domain that stretched from Macedonia to India, he also laid the foundations for Greek to become the common tongue that tied people together in the regions that would later become part of the Roman Empire. In the centuries that preceded the birth of Jesus, the Greek language grew so pervasive that there was no hope of gaining a broad hearing for any idea unless it was recorded in Greek—which is why, no later than the second century B.C., the literature of the Jewish people began to be translated into Greek. And that's also how different texts ended up in different Old Testaments. When the Jewish Scriptures were translated into Greek, the editors included not only Greek renderings of the long-cherished Hebrew and Aramaic Scriptures but also a handful of other compositions from Jewish tradition as well as longer versions of a couple of books. These additional writings are important for understanding the history of the Jewish people, but the Jews never considered them to be the same type of texts as the Hebrew and Aramaic Scriptures. In fact, the author of one of these writings—the first book of the Maccabees—specifically stated that he composed this text during an era when prophetic oracles had ended for a time (1 Maccabees 4:46; 9:27; 14:41).

In addition to incorporating a few additional books, the editors of the Greek Old Testament—a text that came to be known as 'the Septuagint'—rearranged most of the books in the Bible. The result was a sequence somewhat similar to what you might see in many English Old Testaments still today—a sequence that moves from Law to History to Wisdom and Poetry, then finally to the Prophets. The earlier Hebrew and Aramaic Old Testament had been arranged in three sections; in this venerable sequence, the Old Testament moved from:

1. the covenants recorded by Moses that formed the Hebrew people in the first place (the Law of Moses) to

2. a prophetic perspective on Israel's rise and fall as a kingdom (the Prophets) and then to

3. a medley of wisdom literature, priestly histories, and texts for worship and festivals (the Writings).[3]

---

3   4QMMT in the Dead Sea Scrolls also describes a three-part Hebrew and Aramaic canon.

Because the book of Psalms constituted the largest section in the Writings and stood near the beginning of this section, the third segment of the Old Testament was sometimes known as 'Psalms'. Any ancient copy of the Hebrew and Aramaic Old Testament would have been spread over many scrolls, so there was no definitive table of contents of the same type that you might see in a book today. Still, it seems that the books in the Hebrew and Aramaic Old Testament were arranged something like this:

Organization of Hebrew and Aramaic Old Testament	Contents of Hebrew and Aramaic Old Testament
Law of Moses	Genesis, Exodus, Leviticus, Numbers, Deuteronomy
Prophets	Joshua, Judges, Samuel (1 and 2 Samuel), Kings (1 and 2 Kings), Jeremiah, Ezekiel, Isaiah , Book of the Twelve Prophets (Hosea, Joel, Amos, Obadiah, Jonah, Micah, Nahum, Habakkuk, Zephaniah, Haggai, Zechariah, Malachi)

Organization of Hebrew and Aramaic Old Testament	Contents of Hebrew and Aramaic Old Testament
Writings	Ruth, Psalms, Job, Proverbs, Ecclesiastes, Song of Solomon, Lamentations, Daniel, Esther, Ezra-Nehemiah, Chronicles (1 and 2 Chronicles)

Jews were the primary persons who read Hebrew and Aramaic in the first centruy A.D. And so, once the message of Jesus began to multiply among non-Jews, followers of Jesus rarely read the Old Testament in Hebrew and Aramaic. The Greek Septuagint became the Old Testament of the early Christians. In time, so did the additional texts that the editors of the Septuagint had bundled with their translations of the Hebrew and Aramaic Scriptures.

The Greek language did not, however, remain dominant forever. By the fifth century A.D., Latin was rapidly replacing Greek as the primary language for liturgy and literature in the western regions of the Roman Empire. While developing a Latin translation of the Old Testament, a biblical scholar named Jerome pointed out that certain texts in the Septuagint had never been part of the Hebrew and Aramaic Old Testament in the first place. Jerome referred to these compositions as 'Apocrypha', from a Greek word that meant 'hidden' or 'unclear'. Jerome contended that nothing in the Apocrypha should determine any doctrine that Christians believe. Another prominent church leader—Augustine, overseer of churches in the North African city of Hippo—disagreed with Jerome's assessment and demanded that Christians recognize every text in the Septuagint as Scripture. Augustine's opinion prevailed in much of the church and, as a result, apocryphal writings remain in the Old Testaments of the Orthodox and Roman Catholic churches still today, designated as 'deuterocanonical texts'.

Apocryphal Text	Description of Text	Inclusion in Old Testament		
		Jewish and Protestant	Roman Catholic	Orthodox
1 Edras	Similar to Ezra in Hebrew and Aramaic Old Testament, but with some additions	No	No	Yes
Tobit	After being blinded, Tobit sends his son on a quest that results in Tobit being healed	No	Yes	Yes
Judith	Judith defeats the Assyrian general Holofernes	No	Yes	Yes

Apocryphal Text	Description of Text	Inclusion in Old Testament		
		Jewish and Protestant	Roman Catholic	Orthodox
Wisdom of Solomon	Wisdom literature attributed to Solomon	No	Yes	Yes
Wisdom of Sirach	Wisdom Literature, similar to Proverbs	No	Yes	Yes
Baruch	Confession, prayer, and message attributed to Jeremiah's secretary Baruch	No	Yes	Yes
Letter of Jeremiah	Letter attributed to Jeremiah, duplicated in the sixth chapter of Baruch	No	No	Yes
1 Maccabees	Record of Jewish rebellion against the Syrians in second century B.C.	No	Yes	Yes
2 Maccabees	Record of Jewish rebellion against the Syrians in second century B.C.	No	Yes	Yes
3 Maccabees	Record of Jewish rebellion against the Syrians in late third century B.C.	No	No	Yes

RECONSTRUCTING THE BIBLE JESUS KNEW

But what matters most for our purposes is not what Augustine or Jerome thought about the Old Testament. The primary question we're exploring is, 'Which Old Testament texts did *Jesus* receive as uniquely useful and true?'

According to Luke's Gospel, Jesus taught from an Old Testament text that began 'with Moses and all the prophets' (Luke 24:27). As it turns out, the Law of Moses and the Prophets are the first two sections in the Hebrew and Aramaic Old Testament but not in the Septuagint. The editors of the Septuagint text that included the Apocrypha placed most of the prophetic texts later in the Old Testament. A few verses later in Luke's Gospel, Jesus described the Old Testament as a collection that consisted of 'the law of Moses, the prophets, and the psalms' (Luke 24:44). Once again, these words from the resurrected Jesus describe the three-part Hebrew and Aramaic Old Testament—a collection that never included the apocryphal books.

In case it still seems uncertain whether or not Jesus received the Apocrypha as authoritative, consider this: Jesus never cited any apocryphal text as Scripture—and it's not as if Jesus was unaware of the extra texts in the Septuagint![4] By

---

4   Jesus participated in the Festival of Dedication (John 10:22-30), which commemorates an event narrated in 1 Maccabees 4, suggesting that Jesus was aware of the books of the Maccabees; nevertheless, he never quoted or cited any of these texts as Scripture.

the time Jesus began preaching and teaching along the Sea of Galilee, the Septuagint had already been in circulation for more than a century. And yet, even though Jesus cited Old Testament texts dozens of times in his teachings, he never once quoted any apocryphal text.

The first-century followers of Jesus seem to have followed this same pattern. The writers of the New Testament quoted the Greek Septuagint at least two-thirds of the time when they cited Old Testament texts. Yet none of them ever clearly quoted any apocryphal book as Scripture, even though the Septuagint included these additional texts. New Testament authors may have alluded to apocryphal texts from time to time, and they sometimes cited stories from Jewish tradition (see Jude 1:9-10, for example). Yet they never gave any hint that any apocryphal text might belong in the Old Testament.

Disparities do exist in the Old Testaments that you'll find in different churches today. And yet, there are good reasons to recognize only the thirty-nine books that appear in Jewish Bibles and in Protestant Old Testaments as a distinct and unique collection, and I do trust this corpus of texts.[5] My rationale for trusting these thirty-nine texts has nothing to do with church tradition or with any mystical testimony

---

5   The Jewish scribes grouped some books together such that the number of books was considered to be twenty-four or twenty-two, but the texts included in this list were identical to the thirty-nine books in the Protestant Old Testament today. See Timothy Paul Jones, *How We Got the Bible* (Peabody: Rose, 2015), 55.

from the Holy Spirit. I take this collection to be uniquely useful and true on the basis of what was said by a man who returned from the dead. If you trust that the New Testament Gospels rightly reported the teachings and the final fate of Jesus, there is every reason for you to believe these thirty-nine texts as well.

HOW THE RESURRECTION OF JESUS SHAPES THE NEW TESTAMENT

But what about the twenty-seven texts in the New Testament?

Christians today don't typically disagree about which books belong in the New Testament—but that's not because the contents of the New Testament were never contested. For more than a century after the New Testament began to be written, there were differences of opinion about these texts. Unlike the books in the Old Testament, the contents of the New Testament can't be decisively determined by anything that Jesus declared. That's because none of the New Testament was written in the days when Jesus walked the hills of Judea and sailed the Sea of Galilee. The earliest texts in the New Testament were composed two decades after Jesus took a flying trip into the eastern sky from which he has yet to return.

So when *did* Christians agree on the twenty-seven books that appear in the New Testament today? And how was the list finally settled?

According to bestselling biblical scholar Bart Ehrman, the New Testament was in flux at least until the late fourth century A.D. According to Ehrman:

> We are able to pinpoint the first time that any Christian of record listed the twenty-seven books of our New Testament as *the* books of the New Testament— neither more nor fewer. Surprising as it may seem, this Christian was writing in the second half of the fourth century, nearly three hundred years after the books of the New Testament had themselves been written. The author was the powerful bishop of Alexandria named Athanasius. In the year 367 A.D., Athanasius wrote his annual pastoral letter to the Egyptian churches under his jurisdiction, and in it he included advice concerning which books should be read as Scripture in the churches. He lists our twenty-seven books, excluding all others. This is the first surviving instance of anyone affirming our set of books as the New Testament. And even Athanasius did not settle the matter.[6]

Much of what Ehrman has to say here is correct. Questions about a few texts *did* persist well into the fourth century. At the same time, there are some significant aspects of this process that Ehrman's reconstruction omits.

In the first place, it's not as if the contents of the New Testament remained in total flux for centuries, with no foundation to determine which books might be authoritative. Even when the books that became the New Testament

---

6   Bart Ehrman, *Misquoting Jesus* (New York: Harper, 2005), 36.

were being written, a clear standard already existed to determine the type of messages that Christians recognized as authoritative. Words from eyewitnesses of the resurrected Jesus and their close associates carried a distinct and unique authority (see Acts 1:21-26; 15:6–16:5; 1 Cor. 4:1-5; 9:1-12; 15:1-8; Gal. 1:1-12; 1 Thess. 5:26-27). Thus the standard for which books belonged in the New Testament was shaped from the very beginning by the resurrection of Jesus. When witnesses of the resurrected Jesus began to send written exhortations to the churches, these written teachings carried no less authority than their spoken instructions (see, for example, 2 Thess. 3:14). By the end of the first century, apostolic writers were already referring to Paul's writings as 'scriptures' (2 Pet. 3:15-16), and Paul himself had cited a line that later appeared in Luke's Gospel as 'scripture' (1 Tim. 5:18; compare Luke 10:7).

Whether or not the first generations of Christians were right about the writings they selected, their goal at every stage was to recognize and to receive texts that could be connected somehow to eyewitnesses of the resurrected Jesus. The pedigrees of some compositions were well-known, and these texts were accepted immediately. Of the twenty-seven books that comprise the New Testament today, at least nineteen texts—the four Gospels and Acts, Paul's thirteen letters, and the first letter from John—seem to have been recognized as testimony from eyewitnesses or their close associates from the moment that these books first began to circulate. This early fixation on testimony from eyewitnesses can be seen clearly in discussions about what to do with two very popular second-century texts, *The Shepherd* and *Gospel of Peter.*

THE TROUBLE WITH *THE SHEPHERD*

At some point in the second half of the second century A.D., a dispute flared up regarding a popular bit of literature that was circulating under the title *The Shepherd.* Many Christians found this text to be deeply enriching. Within a few years of its release, so many Christians had been encouraged by *The Shepherd* that some believers were urging their churches to include the book among the Scripture readings in their weekly worship gatherings. And that's what brings us to a text known as the Muratorian Fragment.

The Muratorian Fragment includes a rather rough Latin translation of a Greek document from the second century A.D. The original text has been lost, but much of the second-century Greek can be reconstructed from the Latin. The text seems to have originated among a group of church leaders who gathered in the vicinity of Rome. One of the questions these leaders faced had to do with which writings should be included among the texts that Christians read when their churches gathered for worship.

The original text behind the Muratorian Fragment began with a listing that included at least twenty-two of the same texts that you would find in the New Testament today; only Hebrews, James, Peter's two letters, and perhaps John's third letter were missing from the list. The list also mentioned the apocryphal Wisdom of Solomon and a disputed apocalypse that some Christians had ascribed to Simon Peter. However, when it came to *The Shepherd,* the conclusion was that this book should not be included among the books read publicly in the churches. Here's how the church leaders at this gathering summarized their reasons for rejecting *The Shepherd*:

> Hermas composed *The Shepherd* quite recently—in our times, in the city of Rome, while his brother Pius the overseer served as overseer of the city of Rome. So, while it should indeed be read, it cannot be read publicly for the people of the church; it is counted neither among the Prophets (for their number has been completed) nor among the Apostles (for it is after their time).[7]

Notice carefully why these church leaders excluded this book from consideration as an authoritative text in their churches: *The Shepherd* could not be added to the Old Testament because the time of the Old Testament prophets

---

7   'Muratorian Canon in Latin': http://www.earlychristianwritings.com/text/muratorian-latin.html/

had passed ('their number has been completed'), and—with the deaths of the apostles—the era of the eyewitnesses had ended as well ('it is after their time'). There was no appeal to powerful emperors or bishops to determine what to do with *The Shepherd*, and no one suggested piling the books on a table and asking God to drop the false texts on the floor. There was no plan to burn or to ban books that didn't belong in the Bible; in fact, the authors of the Muratorian Fragment said that *The Shepherd* 'should indeed be read' privately. These leaders simply pointed out that the book couldn't serve as an authoritative text that Christians heard when they gathered for worship ('it cannot be read publicly for the people of the church').[8] In the second half of the second century, Christians were already evaluating every text on the basis of a clear and well-established standard, grounded in the eyewitness testimony of the apostles. Since *The Shepherd* was known to have been composed a generation after the last eyewitnesses, this text could not be counted among the Christian Scriptures.

---

8   The practice of reading authoritative texts aloud in the context of communal worship was a distinct feature of second-temple Judaism and Christianity. In other religions, sacred texts were reserved for the priesthood; only in Judaism and Christianity were the texts intended for the people. See Larry Hurtado, *Destroyer of the gods* (Kindle edition; Waco: Baylor University Press, 2016), location 1931.

THE GOSPEL OF THE SKY-HIGH SAVIOR AND THE
TALKING CROSS

A couple of decades after the gathering that produced the text of the Muratorian Fragment, a pastor named Serapion was appointed to lead the church in the city of Antioch in Syria. Soon after becoming the leading pastor in Antioch, Serapion discovered that Christians in the nearby village of Rhossus were in an uproar. The dispute had to do with whether they ought to study a document that had been presented to them 'under Peter's name'. It doesn't seem that the Christians in Rhossus wanted to include this text in their Bibles; they simply wanted to use the book as a devotional text. When Serapion heard about the conflict, he said to them, 'If this is the only thing that seems to produce meanness of soul among you, let it be read.'

When he was finally able to obtain a copy of this mysterious text, Serapion began studying what it had to say and found 'the greater part to be in accordance with the Savior's right word, but with certain things expanded.' According to this text—which came to be known in time as *Gospel of Peter*—Jesus had been crucified and raised from the dead on the third day, in agreement with the New Testament Gospels. But there were also some bizarre expansions in this retelling of the resurrection. According to *Gospel of Peter*, Jesus had stood as high as the sky when he erupted from the tomb; then, after Jesus was raised from the dead, the cross on which he had been crucified started talking.[9]

A sky-high Savior, a talking cross, and a variety of other exaggerations convinced Serapion that the content in *Gospel of Peter* had been falsely ascribed to Simon Peter. And so, Serapion reversed his earlier decision and dashed off a quick note to the church members in Rhossus:

> We accept [the writings of] Peter and the other apostles just as [we would accept] Christ, but, as for those with a name falsely ascribed, we deliberately dismiss them, knowing that no such things have been handed down to us. ... I will hurry to be with you again; expect to see me shortly.[10]

Although Serapion didn't list the writings he used in his comparison, he seems to have possessed biographies of Jesus from earlier generations of Christians. The four New Testament Gospels were so well established by this time that these Gospels almost certainly provided his points of comparison.[11]

9　For the text of *Gospel of Peter,* see Paul Foster, *The Gospel of Peter* (Brill: Leiden, 2010).

10　Serapion of Antioch, as recorded in Eusebius of Caesarea, *Historia Ecclesiastica*, 6:12.

11　Before the end of the second century, Irenaeus of Lyon already saw the four Gospels as an infallible and indivisible set (*Adversus Haereses,* 3:11:8), and Tatian's *Diatessaron* was formed by harmonizing the four Gospels.

Faced with a composition that some had identified as the work of Simon Peter, Serapion compared its claims with trustworthy texts that had been handed down from the apostles and other eyewitnesses. When he compared these texts, he saw significant inconsistencies between *Gospel of Peter* and 'the Savior's right word'. On the basis of this analysis, Serapion concluded that the author could not have been an eyewitness from the apostolic era. As it turns out, Serapion was correct: The language and thought-patterns in *Gospel of Peter* have convinced most contemporary scholars that the book was penned in the first half of the second century, decades after the deaths of the apostles.

This incident from the early third century reveals that early Christians didn't spend centuries pacing the floors and wringing their hands, wondering what sorts of writings they ought to receive as uniquely useful and true. From the very beginning, Christians received the testimonies of the apostles and eyewitnesses of Jesus as authoritative. Not only that, but they also cared deeply about whether or not each book was produced by the person to whom the text was ascribed.

THE EARLIEST SURVIVING LIST OF EVERY NEW TESTAMENT TEXT: AN ORIGEN STORY

So when did Christians arrive at a consensus about the texts in the New Testament?

An initial consensus about nineteen or so books seems to have emerged around the time that these texts first began to circulate. Questions about other documents continued for more than a century—but a consensus about the entirety of the New Testament was well underway no later than the midpoint of the third century. That's when a list of all twenty-seven New Testament books was included in a sermon proclaimed by a scholar known as Origen of Alexandria.

Many have suggested that the first surviving list of all twenty-seven texts originated with Athanasius of Alexandria in 367 A.D. Nothing about the trustworthiness of the New Testament would change if Athanasius had been the first individual to list the same books that appear in the New Testament today. Nevertheless, a more thorough survey of early Christian literature suggests that 367 A.D. was not the point at which all twenty-seven texts were first listed. More than a century before Athanasius of Alexandria cataloged the books of the Bible in his Easter letter, an earlier leader in the Alexandrian church produced a list that included the same twenty-seven books of the New Testament. This leader's name was Origen of Alexandria, and his list preserves the earliest surviving catalog of the twenty-seven texts that comprise the New Testament.[12]

---

12   Origen of Alexandria, *Homilae in Iosuam,* 7:1. For a discussion of the authenticity of this list, see Michael Kruger, 'Origen's List of

Of course, Origen's list didn't end every discussion and dissension about the New Testament. As late as the fourth century A.D., a few church leaders still had doubts about Hebrews, James, Jude, 2 Peter, 2 and 3 John, and Revelation.[13] Nevertheless, the consensus was growing clearer, and the standard for this consensus was already clear. The very fact that fourth-century Christians were still concerned with whether every text could be traced to an apostolic authority reveals that the formation of the New Testament was far from arbitrary. The standard for which texts belonged in the New Testament wasn't the word of any emperor or bishop; it was whether each text could be traced to testimony from men and women who had witnessed the resurrected Jesus in the flesh.

Muratorian Fragment *Late second century*	Origen of Alexandria *Mid-third century*	Eusebius of Caesarea *Early fourth century*
Received	*Received*	*Received*
Matthew	Matthew	Matthew
Mark	Mark	Mark
Luke	Luke	Luke
John	John	John

New Testament Books in *Homilae in Iosuam* 7:1: A Fresh Look', in *Mark, Manuscripts, and Monotheism,* ed. Dieter Roth and Chris Keith (London: T&T Clark, 2015), 99-117.

13 Eusebius of Caesarea, *Historia Ecclesiastica,* 3:3:1-8; 3:24:1-3:25:7.

Muratorian Fragment	Origen of Alexandria	Eusebius of Caesarea
Late second century	*Mid-third century*	*Early fourth century*
Acts	Acts	Acts
Romans	Romans	Romans
1 and 2	1 and 2	1 and 2
Corinthians	Corinthians	Corinthians
Galatians	Galatians	Galatians
Ephesians	Ephesians	Ephesians
Philippians	Philippians	Philippians
Colossians	Colossians	Colossians
1 and 2	1 and 2	1 and 2
Thessalonians	Thessalonians	Thessalonians
1 and 2 Timothy	1 and 2 Timothy	1 and 2 Timothy
Titus	Titus	Titus
Philemon	Philemon	Philemon
1 John	Hebrews[14]	1 Peter
2 John (3 John?)	James	1 John
Jude	1 and 2 Peter	Revelation of
Revelation of John	1, 2, and 3 John	John
Wisdom of	Jude	
Solomon	Revelation of John	

---

14   Origen seems to have accepted a Pauline origin for the concepts in the book of Hebrews, but he believed that someone other than Paul wrote the book. See Eusebius, *Historia Ecclesiastica*, 6:25:11–14.

Muratorian Fragment	Origen of Alexandria	Eusebius of Caesarea
Late second century	*Mid-third century*	*Early fourth century*
Received by some but disputed by others Revelation of Peter	This list matches the list of New Testament books recorded in the Easter letter of Athanasius of Alexandria in 367 A.D.	*Received by some but disputed by others* Hebrews James Jude 2 Peter 2 and 3 John Eusebius, after affirming the Revelation of John as a 'received' book, later acknowledged that Revelation was a text 'which some reject but the rest classify with the received books.'

WAS EVERY TEXT TRACEABLE TO AN EYEWITNESS?

In the end, I do believe that each of the twenty-seven books in the New Testament comes from someone who either saw Jesus personally or who worked closely with an eyewitness of the resurrected Jesus. The Gospels According to Matthew

and John, the book of Revelation, and t[...]
John, James, Peter, and Jude originat[...]
eyewitnesses. The Gospel According to
by a young man who had been Simon Peter's translat[...]
the author of Luke's Gospel was a companion of the apostle
Paul. The book of Hebrews came from someone in the same
circle as Paul's protégé Timothy (Heb. 13:23).

But what if Christians in the first few centuries of the
faith got a few books wrong?

From a wholly human perspective, it's not inconceivable
that a book or two that didn't originate with an eyewitness
might have slipped into the New Testament. The early
church wasn't inerrant, after all. And so, what if John or
Peter or Paul didn't compose every single letter that's ascribed
to them? What if I'm wrong and the Gospel According
to Matthew wasn't really penned by a tax collector who
followed Jesus? Or what if the only texts that were actually
traceable to eyewitnesses were the nineteen or so books that
no one ever questioned?

Even if something of this sort happened, it wouldn't
shake my confidence in the central event of human history
through which God has inaugurated his renewal of the
world, the resurrection of Jesus. That's because evidence
for the resurrection isn't limited to one or two isolated texts
in the New Testament. In fact, every essential belief about
Jesus, about God, and about God's work in the world is

ven throughout multiple texts in a multitude of places in the New Testament. To put it another way, nothing that Christians believe about God requires all twenty-seven books of the New Testament. The New Testament is highly redundant, in a good way, so that no essential teaching or belief is derived from a single text.[15]

Still, when all the evidence is considered, I'm confident that early Christians were right about the books they received as authoritative. I'm not losing any sleep over the implausible possibility that early Christians might have gotten a few of the books in the New Testament wrong. There are substantial reasons to believe that each text in the New Testament comes from the ascribed author and that these authors were eyewitnesses of the resurrected Jesus or individuals closely linked to eyewitnesses.

AIMING THE CANON IN THE RIGHT DIRECTION

Taken together, the sixty-six books of the Old and New Testaments form a 'canon'. I haven't used the word 'canon' up to this point because this wasn't the term that the earliest Christians applied to the books of the Bible. Christians in the first and second centuries had a clear concept of authoritative and non-authoritative texts, but it wasn't until

---

15   John Frame, *The Doctrine of the Word of God* (Phillipsburg: P&R, 2010), 248.

later that the word 'canon' was commonly applied to the list of books that belonged in the Bible.

The word 'canon' can be traced back to an early Semitic root that meant 'tube' or 'reed'. Centuries before the birth of Jesus, this loanword developed into *kanon*, a Greek term that referred to a reed that grows along the Nile River.[16]

So how did a word that refers to a tubular reed end up connected to the books in the Bible? It began when the Greeks began cutting the reeds into specific lengths and using them as measuring sticks. Because these reeds functioned as measuring sticks, the Greek word *kanon* came to denote any tool that set standards and measured limits— and that's how the term came to signify the list of books by which Christians lived their lives. By the mid-fourth century A.D., church leaders such as Athanasius of Alexandria were deploying the word 'canon' to describe the writings that set the standard for Christian faith.

According to some popular atheist writers, early Christians possessed no settled standard by which certain books were received as Scripture and others were rejected. As a result,

---

16 Over the centuries, the Greek word *kanon* picked up an extra 'n' via the Latin *canna* and evolved into a variety of forms that referred to everything from a tubular weapon ('cannon') to tubular pastries and pasta ('cannoli' and 'cannelloni'). These processes may also have produced the word *kannabis* in Greek and *cannabis* in Latin, which described a plant with a tubular stem and other special properties— but it might be better not to explore those properties in a chapter that has already included a 'sky-high Savior'.

the canon must be either a random collection of arbitrarily assembled texts or the result of centuries of careful political manipulations—but such assertions completely overlook the actual historical evidence.[17] Regardless of whether early Christians were right or wrong about the books they chose, records from the second and third centuries reveal clear and consistent reasons why some texts were embraced and others were rejected. These reasons were grounded in eyewitness testimony to the resurrection of Jesus. Early Christians embraced the Old Testament because they worshiped a resurrected Savior who trusted this corpus of texts as divine truth, and the texts in the New Testament were received as authoritative because they could be traced to eyewitnesses of this same Savior. No miracle on a communion table or council of power-hungry pastors formed this canon of sixty-six books. The canon of Scripture was shaped by the historical reality of the resurrection of Jesus.

Matthew	Matthew, follower of Jesus and eyewitness of the resurrected Jesus (Matt. 9:9; 10:3; Acts 1:13)

---

17   See, e.g., Dawkins, *The God Delusion*, 121.

Mark	Mark, traveling companion and translator for Simon Peter (1 Pet. 5:13); 'Mark, in his capacity as Peter's interpreter, wrote down accurately as much as he remembered' (Papias of Hierapolis, early second century)
Luke	Luke, traveling companion with Paul (Col. 4:14; 2 Tim. 4:11); 'Luke—the attendant of Paul—recorded in a book the Gospel that Paul declared' (Irenaeus of Lyon, second century)
John	John, follower of Jesus and eyewitness of the resurrected Jesus (Matt. 4:21; 10:2; Acts 1:13)
Acts	Luke, traveling companion with Paul (Col. 4:14; 2 Tim. 4:11)
Romans, 1 and 2 Corinthians, Galatians, Ephesians, Philippians, Colossians, 1 and 2 Thessalonians, 1 and 2 Timothy, Titus, Philemon	Paul, a later eyewitness of the resurrected Jesus (Acts 9:3-6; 1 Cor. 9:1; 15:8-10)

Hebrews	Based on the author's reference to Timothy (Heb. 13:23), Hebrews was received by early Christians as a composition of Paul or of one of his close associates
James	James, relative of Jesus and eyewitness of the resurrected Jesus (Matt. 13:55; 1 Cor. 15:7; Gal. 1:19; 2:9)
1 and 2 Peter	Simon Peter, follower of Jesus and eyewitness of the resurrected Jesus (Matt. 4:18; 10:2; Acts 1:13)
1 John	John, follower of Jesus and eyewitness of the resurrected Jesus (Matt. 4:21; 10:2; Acts 1:13)
2 and 3 John	John, follower of Jesus and eyewitness of the resurrected Jesus, if written by John the son of Zebedee (Matt. 4:21; 10:2; Acts 1:13); these epistles may have been written by another eyewitness named John, known as 'John the elder', mentioned by Papias of Hierapolis (second century)
Jude	Jude, relative of Jesus (Matt. 13:55; Acts 1:14)

Revelation	John, follower of Jesus and eyewitness of the resurrected Jesus, if written by John the son of Zebedee (Matt. 4:21; 10:2; Acts 1:13); Revelation may have been written by another eyewitness named John, known as 'John the elder', mentioned by Papias of Hierapolis (second century)

RECOMMENDED RESOURCES

Bock, Darrell. *The Missing Gospels.* (Nashville: Thomas Nelson, 2006).

Bruce, F.F. *The Canon of Scripture.* (Downers Grove: InterVarsity, 1988).

Jenkins, Philip. *The Many Faces of Christ.* (New York: Basic, 2015).

Kruger, Michael. *Christianity at the Crossroads.* (Downers Grove: InterVarsity, 2018).

Kruger, Michael. *The Question of Canon.* (Downers Grove: InterVarsity, 2013).

5

How Much of the Bible Must I Trust?

Sometimes, the Bible is a tough text to trust because of the ways that the Bible has been used.

I was reminded of that fact a few months ago when I found myself holding a document penned by men who would have viewed my children as potential property, and they would have quoted the Bible to prove their point.

I was working on a project that required me to research nineteenth-century perspectives on a particular theological topic. Whenever I'm doing historical research, I find it exhilarating to pore over original documents from decades or centuries ago—which might suggest, I readily admit, that I'm at least slightly strange. I want to see with my own eyes the pressure of the pencils on the pages, the notes scrawled in the margins, the faded flourishes of ink from the nibs of long-lost pens. For this particular project, what I needed to examine were early drafts of the first statement of faith from The Southern Baptist Theological Seminary. And that's how I ended up spending a day in the seminary archives, leafing through the original notes and documents from a gathering in April 1858 that brought together the Baptist gentry from the American South who founded this institution.

As I read these papers, I began to paint a picture in my mind of the scene that spring in Greenville, South Carolina—and that's when it struck me that there were almost certainly persons other than the seminary's founders in the room where these drafts were edited. The men who gathered in Greenville were slaveholders. The inkwells for the pens that converted their thoughts into written words were placed on their desks by people they owned. The pitchers of water that moistened their mouths were brought to them by women and men whose prices were listed in ledgers alongside the values of horses and hunting dogs. In that moment of imagination, I caught a glimpse of the ebony and chestnut faces in the unspoken margins of that room, and my eyes brimmed and burned with the painful reminder that the men who produced these papers saw no conflict between Scripture and the subjugation of human beings on the basis of ethnicity. Slavery was—according to one early supporter of the seminary—'an institution of God, and ... we have revealed to us in the Holy Bible clear and overwhelming evidence of its establishment.'[1] And so, here I was, holding a document in my hand from a man who would have looked at the dark flesh of my youngest daughters and at the tight black ringlets of hair that frame their faces and seen potential property. Even worse, he would have grounded his perception in Scripture.

The enslavement of Africans is, unfortunately, far from the first atrocity for which humans have found justification in the pages of Scripture. The good book has also provided an excuse 'for trafficking in humans, for ethnic cleansing, ... for bride-price, and for indiscriminate massacre,' according to a partial list compiled by atheist writer Christopher Hitchens.[2] Beyond this catalog of historical horrors, there is the nagging reality that the Bible appears at times to contradict not only common human kindness but also science, history, and common sense. In some cases, the Bible even seems to contradict itself.

All of this brings us to one of the most difficult aspects of whether or not we should trust the Bible: If I do decide to believe the Bible, how much of the Bible do I need to

---

1   Joseph Emerson Brown, 'Speech of Governor Brown in the Baptist Biennial Convention', *Christian Index* (May 25, 1863), 2. On the use of Scripture to justify slavery in the American South, see Jemar Tisby, *The Color of Compromise* (Grand Rapids: Zondervan, 2019), 80-84.

2   Christopher Hitchens, *God is Not Great* (New York: Hachette, 2009), 102.

believe? And, if it's necessary to trust the Bible in its entirety, what do I do with all the scandals and inconsistencies that seem to be woven through its pages? Abraham Lincoln once commented to a friend concerning the Bible: 'Take all of this book upon reason that you can and the balance on faith, and you will live and die a happier and better man.'[3] But, if we're determined only to trust what is true, how much of the Bible can we actually take on the basis of reason? And how much of it does it make sense to take on faith?

HOW MUCH OF THE BIBLE MUST A BELIEVER BELIEVE?

In a recent *USA Today* opinion piece, a retired pastor made the case that faithfulness to Jesus has never required acceptance of everything the Bible says. 'It's difficult,' he wrote,

> to watch good people (and the churches are full of them) buy into the sincere but misguided notion that being a faithful Christian means accepting everything the Bible teaches. ... The Hebrew and Christian Scriptures did not float down from heaven perfect and without error. They were written by men, and those men made mistakes.[4]

---

3   Rufus Rockwell Wilson (ed.), *Intimate Memories of Lincoln* (Elmira: Primavera, 1945), 22.

4   Oliver Thomas, 'American Churches Must Reject Literalism and Admit We Got It Wrong on Gay People', in *USA Today* (April 29, 2019), https://www.usatoday.com/story/opinion/2019/04/29/american-church-admit-wrong-gays-lesbians-lgbtq-column/3559756002/

From this pastor's perspective, the Bible may provide inspiration for people's lives, but these pearls of inspiration are buried in a field of flawed information that must be corrected on the basis of modern knowledge and experience.

Whenever I read an article of this sort, part of me desperately wishes I could embrace what the author has to say. Many of my conversations with agnostics and atheists would be far easier if I could claim the Bible is true when it tells us about Jesus but not so much when it comes to talking animals or divinely ordained decimations of entire civilizations. The Bible is a tough text to believe at all; what's even more difficult is to trust it all. And yet—despite what this pastor claims—it's simply not possible to follow Jesus faithfully while believing the Bible selectively.

At least a few atheists even recognize this inconvenient but resilient reality. When a Unitarian pastor commented to Christopher Hitchens that she considered herself a Christian but didn't believe in the Bible or the resurrection, the famed atheist's retort was characteristically blunt: 'You're really not in any meaningful sense a Christian.'[5] On this point, the atheist glimpsed the truth more clearly than the pastor. If I select a few portions of the Bible to trust but

5   Marilyn Sewell, 'The Hitchens Transcript', in *Portland Monthly* (December 17, 2009), http://www.portlandmonthlymag.com/arts-and-entertainment/category/books-and-talks/articles/christopher-hitchens/

then treat the rest as nothing more than fabrications, there is no recognizable continuity between my faith and the faith practiced by the earliest generations of Christians.

The earliest Christians received the Old Testament as a text characterized by total truthfulness, and they believed that every part of this text pointed forward to Jesus. According to the author of Acts, the apostle Paul trusted everything that was recorded 'in the law and written in the prophets' (Acts 24:14). Paul himself later wrote that these words were 'inspired by God' (or, 'breathed out by God') and 'profitable' in every part (2 Tim. 3:16). According to the apostle Peter, the Old Testament prophecies were produced as 'men and women moved by the Holy Spirit spoke from God' (2 Pet. 1:21). Before the first century was over, Christians not only received the Old Testament as divine truth but they also placed writings that would become part of the New Testament on the same level as the Old Testament (2 Pet. 3:15-16).[6]

---

6   A significant number of biblical scholars view 2 Peter as a text falsely ascribed to the apostle Peter. However, as Michael Kruger has pointed out: 'Orthodox groups had no need [to ascribe works falsely to apostolic authorities] because their teaching was consistent with the church already and thus they would have no motive to promote it falsely under the name of an apostle.' This line of reasoning is also relevant for Pauline authorship of 1 and 2 Timothy and Titus. See Michael Kruger, 'The Authenticity of 2 Peter', in *Journal of the Evangelical Theological Society* 42 (1999), 671.

Even after the deaths of the apostles, Christians refused to back away from this point of view. 'Nothing unrighteous or counterfeit is written in the Scriptures,' one pastor proclaimed in the late first century A.D. A second-century church leader named Irenaeus of Lyon echoed this sentiment when he said, 'All Scripture is perfectly consistent.' Justin—a philosopher who was later beheaded for his faith—made much the same point with these words: 'I am entirely convinced that no Scripture contradicts another.'[7] These are only a handful of references from dozens of possible examples that reveal what the earliest generations of Christians thought about the Bible. If the New Testament and the words of first- and second-century church leaders rightly represent the faith of the first generations of Christians, these early believers believed the Bible in its entirety. Some portions of the Bible may be awkward and others may be downright weird, but the earliest generations of Christians knew they did not have the option of picking and choosing which parts to believe. Early Christians did not seek to make the claims of Scripture—in the words of John Updike—'less monstrous, for our own convenience.'[8]

---

7   Clement of Rome, *Pros Korinthious*, 45; Irenaeus, *Adversus Haereses*, 2:28:3; Justin, *Dialogi Tryphone*, 65.

8   John Updike, 'Seven Stanzas at Easter', in *Telephone Pole and Other Poems* (New York: Knopf, 1963).

THE RELIABILITY OF THE GOSPELS AND THE
TRUTHFULNESS OF THE WHOLE BIBLE

In the end, despite the many difficulties that I'll unpack in this chapter, I concur with the convictions of these early Christians. When all the facts are known and the texts are interpreted within their cultural and literary contexts, I'm convinced that the Bible—as it was originally written—will turn out to have been accurate in everything it affirms. I believe that the Bible is inerrant and 'free from all falsehood, fraud, and deceit.'[9] And so, in the words of C.S. Lewis, 'I take it as a first principle that we must not interpret any one part of Scripture so that it contradicts other parts.'[10]

If believing the Bible in this way seems absurd to you, you probably have reasons for your doubts, and I hope I'm able to address at least a few of these concerns in this chapter. At the same time, my goal in this chapter is not to convince you that every claim in the entire Bible is true (no single chapter in any book could possibly do that!). My purpose is far less pretentious. I simply want to explore one possible pathway that might reasonably lead someone to the conclusion that the Bible tells the truth.

---

9   For the entire Chicago Statement on Inerrancy, see Norman Geisler (ed.), *Inerrancy* (Grand Rapids: Zondervan, 1980), 493-50.

10   C.S. Lewis, letter to Emily McLay, August 3, 1953, in *The Collected Letters of C.S. Lewis*, ed. Walter Hooper, vol. 3, *Narnia, Cambridge, and Joy*, 1950–1963 (San Francisco: HarperCollins, 2007), 354.

Each time I've found myself wrestling with the question of whether or not the Bible is believable—and there have been several such times in my life—it has been the reliability of the Gospels as historical testimony that has provided a foundation for my belief in the Bible as a whole. My belief in the Bible springs in part from a seedbed of external and internal evidences that support the plausibility of the Gospels as accurate and reliable testimony. This isn't the only possible starting point for believing the Bible is true, but it's the one that has been the most helpful to me.

Regardless of whether or not the New Testament Gospels are divinely inspired or inerrant, it seems more probable than not that they rightly recall the words and works of a man known as Jesus of Nazareth. In everything from the eyewitness origins of the stories in the Gospels to the topography of the lands they describe, these texts exhibit evidence of having been stitched together from reliable testimonies that are traceable to eyewitnesses. If the claims in these texts are generally accurate, a first-century Jew named Jesus claimed divine authority for himself and emerged from a tomb alive three days after he was crucified (Matt. 28:1-20; Mark 8:31; 16:1-8; Luke 24:1-24; John 20:1-23). If the most plausible reconstruction of the evidence suggests that this man was indeed raised from the dead—and I contend that it does—it makes sense to take seriously what the earliest records about him say that he said.

So did Jesus of Nazareth say anything that touches on the question of how much of the Bible should be trusted? As it turns out, he did—and what he said opens the door for receiving the entirety of Scripture as true.

WHAT JESUS SAID ABOUT THE SCRIPTURES

Throughout the Gospels, Jesus explicitly recognized the Old Testament as a reliable and divinely-inspired record of past events (Matt. 12:38-39; 24:37-38; Luke 11:29-32; 17:26-27; John 6:32; 10:35). For Jesus, the truth-telling nature of God his Father guaranteed the truth-conveying nature of Scripture. If Jesus received the Old Testament as a text that was superintended by God and wholly true, it makes sense for those who follow him to do the same.

Now, let's move one step beyond this recognition of the truthfulness of the Hebrew and Aramaic texts that we know today as the Old Testament: If God inspired the collection of words known as the Old Testament prior to the time of Jesus and the apostles, it's not implausible that God might have revealed his truth through written words after Jesus left this planet behind as well—and that's precisely what the first generations of Christians understood that God was doing through the written words of those who had witnessed the resurrected Jesus.

It didn't take early Christians long to reach this conclusion. Before the first century A.D. was over, a saying of Jesus that now appears in the Gospel According to Luke had already been cited by Paul as Scripture alongside a snippet from the Old Testament, and the apostle Peter had already identified the letters of Paul as Scripture (Luke 10:7; 1 Tim. 5:18; 2 Pet. 3:15-16). From the perspective of the first generations of believers, to receive the New Testament books as Scripture was to treat these texts as true in the same way that the Old Testament was true.

In this way, a recognition of the reliability of the New Testament Gospels as historical testimony opens the door to receiving the entire Bible as far more than mere testimony. Here's how James Taylor has summarized this approach:

> If Jesus is the risen Son of God, we can believe what he says. We have good historical grounds for believing that Jesus regarded the Old Testament as God's Word, and therefore we have good reason to believe that it is. In addition, to the extent that we have good historical reasons to think that Jesus really said what the Gospel writers report, we have good reason to regard those dominical sayings as the Word of God. Moreover, Jesus commissioned the apostles to preach the gospel about him to the world. ... Since we have good historical grounds for thinking that the New Testament documents were written by an apostle, someone closely associated with an apostle who would be able reliably to record his teachings, or at least someone who faithfully employed apostolic sources, it

is reasonable to conclude that the New Testament is God's Word.[11]

To follow Jesus is not only to receive the same texts that Jesus received and commissioned but also to trust those texts in the same way he trusted the Scriptures that he read.

You may or may not be satisfied with this line of thinking. Once again, much depends on whether or not you see the resurrection of Jesus as the best explanation for the emergence of a first-century band of believers who refused to stop talking about their resurrected Messiah. Even if you don't find these reasons convincing, one reality should be clear: What I've sketched out here is not circular reasoning, question begging, or blind faith. It is confidence that arises from looking at the Gospels first as testimonies about Jesus and then from examining what their claims might mean not only for the Gospels themselves but also for the rest of the Bible.

WHY THE BIBLE MAY NOT BE AS DIFFICULT TO BELIEVE AS YOU THINK

But what about the difficulties that seem to complicate belief in the Bible? What about the ways the Bible has been deployed to support everything from apartheid and slavery to the decimation of Native Americans and the dehumanization

---

11   James Taylor, *Introducing Apologetics* (Grand Rapids: Baker, 2006), 277-8.

of refugees? And what about the contradictions that seem to tarnish the text of Scripture?

I won't deny that some of these questions have gnawed at my edges of my consciousness at different times in my life. When it comes to the ways that the Bible has been misused as a means of oppression, these difficulties haunt me because they clash with my deep commitment to social equity and racial justice—passions that emerged in me, ironically, precisely because of my commitment to the message of Jesus and the Old Testament prophets. In addition to these struggles with how the text has been misused, there are also apparent inconsistencies in the Bible that I haven't been able to reconcile perfectly.

Nevertheless, I am convinced that trusting the Bible is not nearly as difficult as it may seem to some people. Here's why: Unless you've decided ahead of time that miracles are impossible, *most of the reasons why the Bible seems unbelievable are the result of people trying to do things with the Bible that the Bible was never meant to do.* Not every difficulty falls into this category, but many of the difficulties do. And, whenever any composition is deployed to do things that the author never intended, the results are likely to be disastrous. That does not mean, however, that the composition or the composer is to blame.

If it did, Paul McCartney would have been indicted for murder in the summer of 1969.

WHY PAUL MCCARTNEY WAS NEVER ARRESTED FOR THE MANSON MURDERS

In the autumn of 1968, the Beatles released an eponymous double album with a plain white cover. On side three of this unsurpassed high point of the Beatles' recordings, you'll find a pounding composition from Paul McCartney entitled 'Helter Skelter'. This was the tune that first piqued my interest in the Beatles as a teenager, when U2 performed the song and Bono screamed out, 'This is the song Charles Manson stole from the Beatles. We're stealing it back.'

When Paul McCartney was composing 'Helter Skelter', he may have recognized this was a groundbreaking song that would provide the prototype for rawer and more aggressive music in the future. But what McCartney never could have imagined was how a mentally-deranged young man in southern California would hear this tune. When Charles Manson heard this song he wasn't aware that 'helter skelter' was a circular slide that had become a popular attraction at British amusement parks. What Manson somehow managed to hear in the lyrics was a manifesto for racial war. And so, two weeks after the crew of Apollo 11 returned from the moon in the summer of 1969, Charles Manson instigated a series of murders in an attempt to initiate this bizarre misinterpretation of the Beatles' music. Yet no one ever accused Paul, John, George, or Ringo of being an accessory to any of these crimes.

So, if Charles Manson believed he received his plan for war from Paul McCartney's song, why didn't the state of California demand that the Beatles take the witness stand during Manson's trial?

The reason that the Beatles were never indicted or extradited for these murders is simple: No Beatle was to blame for Manson's misdeeds. Charles Manson used the White Album in a way that the Beatles never intended—and that's worth remembering when you consider all the ways the Bible has been used, abused, and misused over the centuries. Blaming the Bible for misdeeds that have resulted from misconstruing the biblical text would be like indicting Paul McCartney because of how Charles Manson misunderstood 'Helter Skelter'. If the Beatles aren't to blame for the Manson murders, neither is the Bible to blame for the many ways that it's been misconstrued over the centuries. Simply because the Bible has been misunderstood doesn't mean its message must be mistrusted.

With that in mind, let's take a look together at a few facts about the Bible that are frequently overlooked not only by those who don't believe the Bible but also by some who do. Taken together, these facts help us to see that many of the difficulties when it comes to believing the Bible are the result of the Bible being misused.

1. THE BIBLE IS WRITTEN IN DIFFERENT LITERARY GENRES WITH DIFFERENT LEVELS OF PRECISION:

The Bible may be more than mere literature but it's certainly no less than literature. The Bible is, in fact, a literary library that draws together a diverse array of genres and structures and styles. What this means practically is that the Bible is saturated with literary features like hyperbole, poetry, and typology. Source materials throughout the Bible have been rearranged, paraphrased, and selectively emphasized to make particular theological points, and the level of precision varies according to the genre of each text. Cosmic phenomena aren't precisely delineated in modern scientific terms; they're described from the perspective of how they appeared to the observers. And so, the star of Bethlehem was most likely not a star but a comet; no one knows whether the earth actually moved for King Hezekiah or if the king simply saw a shift in the shadow on his sundial; and, it may be that the author of Genesis used a literary framework of six days to provide a poetic description of the formation of the cosmos over billions of years (Gen. 1:1–2:4; 2 Kings 20:8-11; Matt. 2:1-2).[12] None of these literary descriptions

---

12 On the days of creation, see Carl F.H. Henry, *God, Revelation, and Authority: Volume VI: God Who Stands and Stays: Part Two* (Wheaton: Crossway, 1999), chapter 6, and Gordon Wenham, *Genesis 1–15* (Waco: Word, 1987), 39-40; on phenomenological descriptions of astronomical events in the Bible, see Walter Elwell and Philip Comfort (eds), 'Astronomy', in *Tyndale Bible Dictionary*

are errors or deceptions; they're simply the way literature works. As a work of ancient literature composed in a range of different styles, the Bible tells the truth not in the sense of being absolutely precise but in the sense of making good its claims and achieving the measure of focused truth at which its authors were aiming. If you expect the Bible to be more precise than it's intended to be, you may think there's an error in the Bible when there's really no error at all.[13]

2. *THE BIBLE RIGHTLY RECORDS WHAT HAPPENED EVEN WHEN WHAT HAPPENED WASN'T RIGHT:*

The Bible was never intended to provide a pristine list of human triumphs to celebrate or praiseworthy acts to imitate. This literary library is packed with stories that will never show up in any children's story book. That's mostly because parents tend to avoid purchasing books for their progeny that describe human sacrifices, bodily dismemberment, and other acts that could cause severe emotional trauma. People in the Bible are a mess, for the most part. There is, in fact, only one person in the entire Bible who didn't fail, and he ended up on a cross. As Homer Simpson once commented

---

(Wheaton: Tyndale House, 2001), 126; on the star of Bethlehem, see Colin Nicholl, *The Great Christ Comet* (Wheaton: Crossway, 2015).

13 For an early Christian treatment of the Gospels as literature, see Augustine of Hippo, *De Consensu Evangelistarum.*

after reading the Scriptures on *The Simpsons*, 'Talk about a preachy book. Everybody's a sinner! Except this one guy.'

More often than not, the historical narratives in the Bible were written to reveal humanity's failures, and many of these stories seem to have been meant to lead us to mourn and lament. When Abraham's nephew Lot impregnates both of his daughters while glutted on wine, the author of Genesis is presenting Lot as a depraved coward to despise, not as a paragon to imitate (Gen. 19:8, 30-38). When Jephthah sacrifices his daughter as a burnt offering, his sacrifice is never praised; instead, this distorted understanding of divine law leads to an annual liturgy of lamentation (Judg. 11:40). In the most horrific story in all of Scripture, a religious leader hacks his concubine into pieces after allowing her to be raped and beaten to the point of unconsciousness (Judg. 19:25-30)—but the point of this narrative is clearly to provoke mourning at the callous violence of the Israelites during this dark period in their history.

These texts and others like them were woven into the Word of God to trigger shock and godly grief. And yet, these are the very texts that Richard Dawkins misconstrues to portray the Old Testament as an 'ethical disaster area' in which such acts are treated with approval.[14] A legislator is not, however, endorsing a crime simply because she describes the crime

---

14   Dawkins, *The God Delusion*, 284.

in detail in a law that she writes to prohibit the crime. In the same way, the biblical authors weren't approving heinous acts simply because they described them in the books they composed and compiled. In fact, the exact opposite is true. These narratives were meant to commemorate the pain of the exploited and to prevent certain events from ever happening again.

'God save me from the day when stories of violence, rape, and ethnic cleansing inspire within me anything other than revulsion,' Rachel Held Evans reflected in her book *Inspired*. 'I don't want to become a person who is unbothered by these texts.'[15] I have frequently found myself disagreeing with Rachel Held Evans, but she's not wrong to be bothered by these stories. In certain biblical narratives, to search for praiseworthy morals is to miss the point completely. Some portions of the Bible were penned, in part, to provoke revulsion. This revulsion should not, however, be directed toward the Bible itself but toward the depravity within each of us that produces such inhumanity.

3. THE BIBLE WORKS BEST WHEN IT'S UNDERSTOOD IN ITS OWN CONTEXT BEFORE BEING APPLIED IN ANOTHER CONTEXT:

If you believe the Bible is an inspired Word from God, it's tempting to read the Bible as if it's a compendium of wise

---

15   Rachel Held Evans, *Inspired* (Nashville: Nelson, 2018), 79.

maxims that you can drop directly into your everyday life—sort of like the sayings in *Poor Richard's Almanack,* except compiled by the God of Israel instead of Benjamin Franklin. And yet, the books in the Bible were composed and compiled in a broad range of genres and locations over the span of more than a thousand years. Due to this distance between the biblical cultures and our own, it doesn't typically work to apply these texts to our contexts without first understanding them in their original contexts—but that hasn't kept well-meaning people throughout history from trying to skip this crucial step.

Much of the time, bypassing the original context results in relatively harmless misapplications of a text. When faced with poverty and persecution, Paul declared his confidence in Christ with these words: 'I can do all things through him who strengthens me' (Phil. 4:13). Producers of Christian kitsch have stripped this text from its context and turned it into a slogan for cat posters and coffee mugs. In the process, they've stretched Paul's message far past anything in the original context. Still, I doubt that anyone's confidence in the Bible has been decimated because they saw Paul's words to the Philippians printed in neon pink alongside a picture of a cat clinging to a branch.

In other instances, ignoring the original context of a biblical text results in confusion because of a failure to distinguish between the two testaments. The laws given to

Moses in the first section of the Bible—the Old Testament—were never meant to be permanent or universal (Gal. 3:23-25; Heb. 8:5-7, 13; 10:8-9). These laws provided a temporary picture that pointed forward to God's work in the New Testament. Today, this collection of texts has been fulfilled in Jesus, and the Old Testament laws are not binding on believers in the same way that they were among the ancient Israelites (Matt. 5:17).[16] And yet, when making the point that same-sex sexual relationships are incompatible with faithfulness to Jesus, Christians frequently cite Old Testament texts such as this one: 'If a man lies with a male as with a woman, both of them have committed an abomination' (Lev. 20:13). One of the many problems with citing this verse is that the laws in this section of Leviticus also forbid everything from beard-trimming to planting two different crops in the same field (Lev. 19:19, 27)—which raises the very legitimate question of why, if these texts are binding on Christians today, more pastors aren't preaching against shaving your beard or growing green beans and aubergine in the same garden. It's true that same-sex sexual

---

16 Christians who agree about the authority of Scripture disagree about the role of the Old Testament law today. Still, regardless of one's perspective, the Old Testament laws are not binding on believers in Jesus in the same way that they were on the Israelites in the Old Testament. See Chad Brand (ed.), *Perspectives on Israel and the Church* (Nashville: B&H, 2015), and Stanley Gundry (ed.), *Five Views on Law and Gospel* (Grand Rapids: Zondervan, 2010).

relationships are incompatible with the teachings of the Bible. Yet the laws in Leviticus aren't the best place to begin when making that case, and there's really no need to start with these laws in the first place. Jesus himself made it clear in the New Testament that the only faithful possibilities for the sexual lives of his followers are either celibacy or heterosexual marriage (Matt. 19:4-12), and Paul reiterated that same point in his letters to the early churches (Rom. 1:26-27; 1 Cor. 6:9; 1 Tim. 1:10). To start this discussion today with a single text from Leviticus is to try to make the Old Testament law do something that it wasn't meant to do.

In a handful of cases throughout history, failing to understand biblical texts in their original contexts has resulted in cultural systems that have had deeply destructive consequences—and that brings us back to where this chapter began, with the Southern gentry who saw their ownership of African-American slaves as a divinely-ordained right. These men read verses in their Bibles that mentioned slavery, and they applied these texts to the systems of slavery that they knew without acknowledging the radical distinctions between the biblical context and their own. Here's how Tim Keller has summarized the distinctions that separated these systems:

> In the first-century Roman empire, when the New Testament was written, there was not a great difference between slaves and the average free person. Slaves were

not distinguishable from others by race, speech, or clothing. They looked and lived like most everyone else and were not segregated from the rest of society in any way. From a financial standpoint, slaves made the same wages as free laborers, and therefore were not usually poor. ... Most important of all, very few slaves were slaves for life. ...

By contrast, New World slavery was much more systematically and homogeneously brutal. It was 'chattel' slavery, in which the slave's whole person was the property of the master—he or she could be raped or maimed or killed at the will of the owner. In the older bond-service or indentured servanthood, only slaves' productivity—their time and skills—were owned by the master, and only temporarily. African slavery, however, was race-based, and its default mode was slavery for life.[17]

This isn't to suggest that slavery was somehow desirable in the New Testament; if it had been, Paul wouldn't have urged Christian slaves to purchase their freedom (1 Cor. 7:21-23). But the default mode of this form of slavery was never lifelong or racially-based. What's also distinct about the systematic enslavement of Africans was that this form of chattel slavery would have been impossible without the theft of human beings for profit—and that act is explicitly identified in the New Testament as a vile evil. In one of his letters to a young

---

17 Timothy Keller, *The Reason for God* (New York: Dutton, 2008), 110.

pastor in Ephesus, the apostle Paul positioned this offense alongside murder, perjury, and the practice of homosexuality: 'The law is laid down not for the innocent but ... for those who kill their father or mother, for murderers, fornicators, sodomites, *slave traders*, liars, perjurers, and whatever else is contrary to the sound teaching' (1 Tim. 1:9-10, emphasis added). The term translated 'slave traders' in this text can scarcely imply anything other than the taking of persons from their native land for the purpose of profiting from their enslavement.

The men who met in Greenville in 1858 to produce a statement of faith for their seminary studied the same Scriptures that I trust today. And yet, they did not interpret the Scriptures in such a way that these truths could convict them in their context. As a result, they twisted the Bible to make it do something it was never intended to do, and they failed to see a sin in themselves that the apostle Paul would have glimpsed immediately. I cannot excuse them, but neither do I despise them. Instead, I am driven to consider if there are similar shortfallings in my own thinking today— if there are, perhaps, areas in my thought where my own context has so deeply blinded me that I am not convicted by a truth that God has revealed in his Word.

WHAT ABOUT CONTRADICTIONS IN THE BIBLE?

Most of the difficulties with trusting the truthfulness of Scripture fade away when we stop trying to make the Bible do things that it was never meant to do—but not all of the difficulties vanish when the Bible begins to be rightly interpreted. Even after carefully interpreting texts as literary texts in their original contexts, there are times when the Bible seems to contradict history, common sense, or even itself.

If I'm honest with you, I must admit that, even after decades of studying the Bible, there are a few incongruities that I've never been able to reconcile in a way that completely satisfies me. One of these incongruities has to do with something that Jesus said during a confrontation with the Pharisees. According to Jesus, King David 'entered the house of God, when Abiathar was high priest' (Mark 2:26). The problem is that—according to the books of Samuel— the priest at that time wasn't Abiathar at all; it was Abiathar's father Ahimelech (1 Sam. 21:1-6).

Another difficulty shows up in Luke's account of the birth of Jesus. According to Luke, the census that brought Mary and Joseph to Bethlehem took place 'while Quirinius was governor of Syria' (Luke 2:1-2). And yet, external historical sources suggest that Publius Sulpicius Quirinius hadn't yet been appointed legate governor of Syria when Jesus was born. It seems that nearly a decade separates the birth of

Jesus from the time when Quirinius received his imperial appointment as governor of Syria.

And then there's a bizarre text in Genesis 38 that too many people ignore. According to this text, a woman named Tamar was giving birth to twins. While Tamar was in labor, one of the twins,

> put out a hand; and the midwife took and bound on his hand a crimson thread, saying, 'This one came out first.' But just then he drew back his hand, and out came his brother. ... Afterward his brother came out with the crimson thread on his hand. (Gen. 38:28-30)

I've never personally given birth to a child. I am, however, sufficiently familiar with the process to know that, when a child is being born, the birth canal is a one-way street with only one lane. Given that fact, I have serious doubts about whether it's possible for one newborn to reach out his hand long enough to wave at the midwife and receive a red thread but then to reverse his course in such a way that he ends up being born second instead of first.

So what do I do with these incongruities?

Imagine that you have a close friend whom you've trusted for many years. You and this friend have weathered many challenges together, and you have every reason to trust your friend's honesty and integrity. But then, one day, your friend makes a series of statements that seem contradictory while talking about a topic that your friend knows and understands well.

What do you do?

Most likely, your first assumption is not that your friend has suddenly transformed into a double-crossing chronic liar. You've spent too many years together, trusting each other, for that to be your first response. The first possibility that crosses your mind will probably be that your friend's two statements somehow fit together in a way you don't yet understand.

When I face an incongruity in the Bible, I respond with the same attitude—except that I view the Bible with a more profound confidence than I find in any friend, because my confidence in the Bible is grounded not merely in my own personal experiences but in the testimonies of those who saw the resurrected Jesus and in the deeper testimony of God himself in Jesus. And so, when I see an apparent contradiction in the Bible, I assume either that the statements fit together in a way I don't yet understand or that one of the solutions with which I'm not yet satisfied is the right solution after all. Given the historical truth that I find in the rest of the Bible—and particularly in the Gospels—there are good reasons to think that this trusted friend isn't lying to me.

And so, when I read Mark 2:26, I recognize that the wording that's translated 'when' in the clause 'when Abiathar was high priest' can mean 'in the days of' and point to a broader time than one man's lifetime. When I study Luke 2:2, I know the clause rendered 'while Quirinius was governor of Syria' could be read 'when Quirinius was commanding Syria,' which may suggest that Quirinius managed a census in this region several years before he actually became governor; it's also not impossible to translate the text 'this was the census before Quirinius was commanding Syria,' though the Greek grammar would be awkward in this reading. When I read about the crimson thread on the newborn's wrist, I have no natural explanation, and I conclude that my friend the Bible is a little weird sometimes—and I suspect that what happened to Tamar was a miracle in which God blessed the twin that no one expected him to bless in much the same way that he chose Jacob over Esau (Gen. 25:23). None of these solutions deals comprehensively with every conceivable question, but—seen in the larger context of the confidence of Jesus in the Old Testament and the character of the God who raised Jesus from the dead—these solutions are sufficient for now.

'IT IS A FACT TO WHICH WE CAN CALL WITNESSES'

The Bible is a difficult book to believe.

And yet, I do believe it, and this confidence is not without evidence. As I consider the evidence that reveals the coherence of this confidence, I recall the words that G.K. Chesterton wrote nearly a century ago:

> In answer to the historical query of why [the Christian faith] was accepted and is accepted, I answer for millions of others in my reply; because it fits the lock, because it is like life. It is one among many stories; only it happens to be a true story. ... This is the sort of truth that is hard to explain because it is a fact; but it is a fact to which we can call witnesses.[18]

'It is a fact to which we can call witnesses,' Chesterton said—and indeed it is. A man who died was raised to life, and this event was not hidden from human view. People saw him alive, and those who saw this man alive became witnesses who were more willing to let go of their own lives than to deny what they had seen. This man who was raised from death to life trusted the Old Testament as divine truth, and the texts that we know now as the New Testament were traceable to eyewitnesses that he commissioned. This array of witnesses reveals the rationality of embracing the biblical canon as God's unerring Word. You may not find this line of reasoning to be convincing, but I do hope you see that it is not unreasonable.

---

18   Gilbert Keith Chesterton, *The Everlasting Man* (repr. ed., New York: Image, 1955), 249, 289.: Retrieved March 30, 2006, from http://www.dur.ac.uk/martin.ward/gkc/.

The more I have wrestled with each possibility over the past three decades, the more I am convinced that—though there is much that I do not know and there are a handful of disparities that I still cannot reconcile—Christian faith is no dead end. At some point where the horizons of history and faith ever so gingerly embrace, I still find myself unable to escape this simple conviction: The tomb was empty because what appeared to be the end of the story was actually the birth of a new beginning, because death turned into life, because what was least probable of all became possible and real and true.

CONCLUDING REFLECTIONS

If we live in a world where it is possible for a divine power to bring a dead man back to life, a divinely inspired collection of texts is not an unreasonable possibility.

By this point, I hope it's clear to you that there is evidence for such a world. In a book as brief as this one, there has only been sufficient space to present a minuscule fraction of these evidences. And yet, if you have already decided that such a world is impossible, I suspect that more evidence wouldn't make much difference in what you believe. The foundational question for you has to do with whether you're willing to admit that the cosmos in which we live is a place where there is space for both natural and supernatural powers.

If you have already decided that there is no space for the supernatural in your worldview, the real reason probably has little to do with the evidence and much to do with what you desire. It's quite conceivable that you don't want to live in a world that brims and seethes with the presence of God, because a God-filled cosmos would demand a response of obedience and surrender that you don't desire to give. As long as you remain unwilling to admit the possibility of a universe where there are more powers at work than mere physical forces, you will find some reason to reject the possibility of the type of God who would create such a cosmos.

But perhaps you find yourself open to the possibility of a cosmos where a power greater than any material reality might return a man from death to life. If you are willing to consider the possibility of such a place, this very willingness may be a sign of divine grace. It is grace alone that opens the door of escape from our delusion of a godless cosmos, and the power that draws us through this door is a power greater than ourselves. If you are open to that possibility, my encouragement to you is simply this: read the four New Testament Gospels for yourself, with an open and receptive mind. When you reach the end, read them again. What you will find in the Gospels is the radical claim that the crucified Jesus took the punishment that you and I deserve for our unbelief. And yet, this death could not hold him because he was more than any mere man. Through his life, death, and resurrection, the reign of God has been revealed on the earth, and anyone who turns to him in faith can be reconciled to God and become part of God's renewal of his world. As you read the Gospels, consider carefully whether the Jesus described in these ancient pages might really be alive and—if he is—what your response to him should be.

RECOMMENDED RESOURCES

Cowan, Steven, and Terry Wilder (eds). *In Defense of the Bible.* (Nashville: B&H, 2013).

Mohler, R. Albert. 'When the Bible Speaks, God Speaks', in *Five Views on Biblical Inerrancy.* ed. James Merrick and Stephen Garrett. (Grand Rapids: Zondervan, 2013), 29-58.

Plummer, Robert. *40 Questions about Interpreting the Bible.* (Grand Rapids: Kregel, 2010).

Poythress, Vern Sheridan. *Inerrancy and the Gospels.* (Wheaton: Crossway, 2012).

Poythress, Vern Sheridan. *Inerrancy and Worldview.* (Wheaton: Crossway, 2012).

Appendix

How Accurately Was the Bible Copied?

Note to the reader: This appendix is more technical than the rest of the book, but it may be helpful to you if you have ever wondered whether the Bible was copied accurately, particularly if you or a friend has read Misquoting Jesus *by Bart Ehrman.*

L et's suppose that you wanted to purchase another copy of this book.

Actually, while we're thinking such happy thoughts, let's suppose you needed a thousand additional copies of *Why Should I Trust the Bible?* As soon as you charge those thousand volumes to your credit card and the books arrive at your house, you'll be ready to move on to the next paragraph.

As you lovingly smell the pages and peruse each volume of these thousand freshly-purchased copies of *Why Should I Trust the Bible?* that now adorn your living room, you may begin to notice a peculiar pattern: *Each copy of the book is pretty much identical.* The same words appear in the same places on the same pages in every copy of this book.

Then again, you might *not* see this pattern as peculiar, because it seems perfectly normal to you—but the reason this pattern seems normal is because the fifteenth century was already in the past by the time you and I were born.

For most of human history, such uniformity in different copies of the same scroll or book would have struck readers as strange. That perception didn't begin to change until the fifteenth century, when a man named Johannes Gutenberg perfected a press that printed books using a new type of type. Each letter that Gutenberg forged for his press was movable and molded from a long-lasting metal alloy. This allowed books to be typeset more quickly and duplicated more uniformly than ever before. Prior to the widespread adoption of Gutenberg's press, metal-smiths sometimes forged full-page plates to print books, and woodworkers might have carved entire manuscript pages for a printing press—but such plates were inefficient to produce, and they wore out quickly. And so, until the rise of the movable metal-type printing press, most texts continued to be copied by hand.

Whenever a book is copied by hand, different copies of the same book will never be identical—and it's not simply the style or the spacing of the letters that will vary.

Human copying capacities are imperfect because humans are imperfect. What's more, human beings are quite capable of convincing themselves that they have the capacity to improve the texts that they're copying. And so, words and phrases inevitably end up changed. That's why a handmade copy will never be an exact copy.

So what does that mean for the Bible?

Think about it for a moment: For more than a millennium, the words of the Bible were copied by hand in an age that predated eyeglasses and electric lights. If other texts have been modified over generations of copying, doesn't that mean the Bible has been changed as well? And, if the Bible has been altered over the centuries, how can anyone trust what the Bible has to say, even if the initial editions of each book may have told the truth?

WAS JESUS MISQUOTED?

Few people other than biblical scholars seem to have concerned themselves with these questions prior to the early twenty-first century. All of that began to change around 2005 when a book entitled *Misquoting Jesus: The Story Behind Who Changed the Bible and Why* unexpectedly rushed to the upper reaches of the bestseller lists. After comedian Jon Stewart promoted *Misquoting Jesus* as 'a helluva book', this treatise about the text of the Bible became a number-one bestseller on Amazon.com—quite a feat for a book that expends most of its pages exploring the rather tedious history of biblical manuscripts.[1] The author of this unexpected blockbuster book was New Testament scholar Bart Ehrman.

Misquoting Jesus takes a less-than-cheery perspective on the reliability of those many generations of hand-copied manuscripts. Here's how Bart Ehrman describes the condition of the biblical texts in *Misquoting Jesus*:

> We don't have the originals [of the biblical manuscripts]. ... What we have are copies made later—much later. ... These copies differ from one another in so many places that we don't even know how many differences there are. Possibly it is easiest to put it in comparative terms: there are more differences among our manuscripts than there are words in the New Testament. ... We have only error-ridden copies, and the vast majority of these are centuries removed from the originals. ... If one wants to insist that God inspired the very words of scripture, what would be the point if we don't *have* the very words of scripture? In some places, ... we simply cannot be sure that we have reconstructed the text accurately. It's a bit hard to know what the words of the Bible mean if we don't even know what the words are.[2]

According to the cover copy for *Misquoting Jesus*, 'many of our cherished biblical stories and widely held beliefs concerning the divinity of Jesus, the Trinity, and the divine

---

1   Daniel Wallace, 'The Gospel According to Bart', in *Journal of the Evangelical Theological Society* 49 (June 2006), 327.

2   Ehrman, *Misquoting Jesus*, dust jacket, 7, 10-11.

origins of the Bible itself stem from both intentional and accidental alterations by scribes.' Some of the changes that copyists have made are—Ehrman claims—so earth-shaking that they have altered 'the interpretation of an entire book' of the Bible.[3]

Despite these rather dire assessments of the biblical text, I must admit that I appreciate most of what *Misquoting Jesus* has to say. That's partly because, even though I disagree strongly with Ehrman's conclusions, he's helped people to see that this is an issue that can't be ignored. I also appreciate *Misquoting Jesus* because I was raised in churches that lied to me about this very topic. According to what I was taught as a teenager, the Bible has been perfectly preserved with no copying variants in a lineage of manuscripts known as the 'Textus Receptus', from which the King James Version of the Bible was translated. These claims that I heard from fundamentalist pulpits were—I learned years later—completely false. The original manuscripts of the Bible decayed into dust centuries ago, and not one ancient manuscript agrees in every detail with any of the others. *Misquoting Jesus* helps to dispel this flawed perception of perfectly preserved manuscripts.

At the same time, significant problems and exaggerations pop up throughout *Misquoting Jesus*. The variants that Bart

---

3   Ehrman, *Misquoting Jesus*, dust jacket, 132.

Ehrman describes have had far less effect on the text than his book seems to suggest. The biblical manuscripts weren't copied with perfect precision, but neither was their message lost in transmission. Despite the presence of multiple textual families and hundreds of thousands of copying variants, the surviving manuscripts adequately—albeit imperfectly—preserve the message of the Old Testament that Jesus trusted and the New Testament that eyewitnesses of his resurrection and their close associates composed. Comparison of biblical texts across the ages suggests that generation after generation of copyists replicated the biblical texts with sufficient accuracy to maintain the same message that was present in the initial manuscripts.

PROCESSES THAT PRODUCED THE BIBLICAL MANUSCRIPTS

When it comes to the Old Testament, a scribal clan known as the 'Sopherites' (from the Hebrew *saphar,* 'to count') emerged early in Israel's history and oversaw the replication of sacred texts. These scribes and their heirs developed detailed guidelines to preserve the Hebrew and Aramaic Scriptures.[4] Near the end of the fifth century A.D., a group of Jewish scholars known as the 'Masoretes' (from the Hebrew *masorah,* 'tradition') standardized and expanded

---

4   Frederic Kenyon, *Our Bible and the Ancient Manuscripts,* rev. ed. (New York: Harper, 1958), 34-5, 78-9.

these guidelines.[5] The Masoretes counted how many words and letters belonged in every book in their Bible, and they even knew which word and what letter should stand at the exact center of every book. Over time, they developed an entire series of marginal markings and vowel points to preserve the ancient readings of the texts that they received.

As far as anyone knows, Christian copyists didn't count the words or letters in the texts they copied—but they quickly developed well-ordered informal practices for preserving their sacred texts. A significant number of early Christian copyists seem to have been trained scribes whose handwriting reflected the style of ordinary documents of their day; the result was a script that is consistent and clear but unadorned.[6] Much like earlier Jewish scribes, Christian copyists included spacing patterns and breathing marks in the texts to assist those who read the Scriptures aloud in weekly worship gatherings.[7] Early fragments of the New

---

5　Paul Wegner, *The Journey From Texts to Translations* (Grand Rapids: Baker, 2004), 172-7.

6　Alan Mugridge, *Copying Early Christian Texts* (Tübingen: Mohr-Siebeck, 2016), 147.

7　P. Ryl. 457 (fragment of John's Gospel, second or third century A.D.) and P. Ryl. 458 (pre-Christian fragment of Deuteronomy, second century B.C.) exhibit similar patterns which indicate that, though at least two centuries separate these texts, the copyists followed similar conventions with Jewish roots to produce texts suitable for liturgical usage. Cf. C.H. Roberts, 'Two Biblical Papyri in the John Rylands Library Manchester', in *Bulletin of the John Rylands Library* 20 (1936), 226-7. See also Victor Martin,

Testament also exhibit distinct patterns of abbreviating words such as 'God', 'Lord', 'Jesus', and 'Christ' that are unique to Christian texts, suggesting that early Christian copyists noticed and followed certain shared copying practices.[8] Early fragments from Matthew's Gospel reveal that early readers of the New Testament made corrections when manuscripts had been miscopied.[9] These ancient emendations weren't always correct, but they do show a capacity and a willingness to compare texts to conserve the best readings. While some copyists may have been loose and fluid in their copying, the primary concern of the women and men who copied the Scriptures seems to have been to preserve the words that they received.[10]

Papyrus Bodmer II, Evangile de Jean chap. 1–14 (Cologne-Geneva: Bibliotheque Bodmer, 1956), 18-21.

8   These unique abbreviations (known as *nomina sacra*, 'sacred names') appear in third-century texts such as P. Oxy. 4401 (P101), P. Oxy. 4445 (P106), P. Oxy. 4447 (P108), P. Oxy. 4449 (P110), P. Oxy. 4495 (P111), P. Oxy. 4497 (P113), P. Oxy. 4498 (P114), and P. Oxy. 4499 (P115). New Testament texts that might have been copied in the second century A.D. are too fragmentary to know for certain whether *nomina sacra* may have been present. In some cases, ἄνθρωπος was treated as a *nomen sacrum,* suggesting that the practice was not formally regulated; it was inferred by copyists from the texts they saw. If formal instruction was involved, this instruction was limited in scope. See Larry Hurtado, *The Earliest Christian Artifacts* (Grand Rapids: Eerdmans, 2006), 122-33.

9   See, e.g., P. Oxy. 4403 (P103) and P. Oxy. 4405 (portion of P77).

10 The rise of religious communities for women in the Middle Ages provided a context in which women produced manuscripts in scriptoria. At least as early as the eighth century A.D., women in

But the most important question for our purposes isn't whether these copyists *intended* to preserve the text; it's whether or not they *succeeded*. To find out how well the copyists preserved the text, let's begin by taking a quick trip to a series of limestone cliffs near the northwestern corner of the Dead Sea.

A FLOCK, A ROCK, AND A CAVE FILLED WITH SCROLLS

Until the mid-twentieth century, no one knew for certain whether the text that the Masoretes had preserved was an accurate representation of earlier Hebrew and Aramaic texts of the Old Testament. The oldest known copy of the entire Old Testament was a Masoretic manuscript produced more than a thousand years after the initial texts were written.

But then, in 1947, a young shepherd discovered the Dead Sea Scrolls, and that changed everything.

Muhammed edh-Dhib had lost his sheep, and he didn't know where to find them—or at least that's the story that circulated afterward. According to one version of the local legend, Muhammed tossed a rock into a cave, hoping to hear the bleating of his lost flock when the rock landed. What he heard instead was the shattering of pottery. It's possible that

the Western churches participated in the copying and preservation of religious texts. See Rosamond McKitterick, 'Nuns' Scriptoria in England and Francia in the Eighth Century', in *Francia* 19 (1992), 1-35; Anita Radini, et al., 'Medieval Women's Early Involvement in Manuscript Production Suggested by Lapis Lazuli Identification in Dental Calculus', in *Science Advances* 5 (2019), 1-8.

the sixteen-year-old shepherd was seeking his goats when he ran across the desert cave. It's also conceivable that he was hunting for tombs that might contain valuable artifacts—no one knows for certain. Regardless of what Muhammed was actually looking for when he located those pottery jars, what he found inside the jars would impact the world long after his flocks were forgotten.

What Muhammed edh-Dhib discovered in the winter of 1947 were the first of the Dead Sea Scrolls. In the decade that followed the initial discovery of seven scrolls, nine hundred or so additional fragments and scrolls were located in nearby caves. More than two hundred of these texts were manuscripts of the Old Testament copied before the birth of Jesus.

When the scrolls and fragments were analyzed, it became clear that the Old Testament text had remained far more stable over the centuries than many scholars had imagined. One scroll of Isaiah discovered among the Dead Sea Scrolls was produced at least a century before the time of Jesus. Yet the wording of this copy of Isaiah was virtually identical to the Masoretic texts that were copied a thousand years later. The remainder of the Dead Sea Scrolls did reveal a variety of versions and copying variations in other Old Testament texts. And yet, even in these texts, none of the changes challenged anyone's overall understanding of the Bible or any of the beliefs that have been derived from these texts.

What the Dead Sea Scrolls revealed is that the processes practiced by the scribes of Israel had preserved the text of the Old Testament with exceptional accuracy.

MORE VARIANTS THAN THERE ARE WORDS? YES—AND NO

The New Testament manuscripts include far more variants than the Old Testament texts, partly because far more manuscripts of the New Testament have survived. And yet, these same manuscripts also reveal a text that's remained remarkably stable over the centuries. Fragments from the second and third centuries generally confirm the text that's found in complete manuscripts of the New Testament from the fourth and fifth centuries.[11] When variations in the text of Acts are compared in the two most dissimilar 'families' of New Testament manuscripts, the level of consensus between the text types is 92%; a similar comparison of the letters of James, Peter, John, and Jude yields 93% agreement, leaving very little of the text in question.[12]

---

11 Peter Head, 'Some Recent Published New Testament Papyri from Oxyrhynchus', in *Tyndale Bulletin* 51 (2000), 16-18.

12 According to Gregory Lanier, the undivided Byzantine text fully agrees with the *Editio Critica Major* text of Acts, James, 1 and 2 Peter, 1, 2, and 3 John, and Jude 94 percent of the time, even though these two text forms should be the most diametrically opposed. For variation units as defined by the *Editio Critica Major*, the rate of agreement between the two most dissimilar textual families is 92 percent for Acts and 93 percent for James, 1 and 2 Peter, 1, 2, and 3 John, and Jude. See Gregory Lanier, 'Dating Myths, Part 2', in *Myths and Mistakes about New Testament Textual Criticism*,

How is it, then, that Bart Ehrman claims 'there are more differences among our manuscripts than there are words in the New Testament'? And do these differences actually include 'lots of significant changes'?[13]

What Ehrman claims in *Misquoting Jesus* is partly correct. There *are* more differences spread across all the manuscripts than there are words in a single Greek New Testament. The Greek New Testament includes around 138,000 words, and there are around a half-million copying variants in the Greek texts.[14] And yet, what Ehrman says is also misleading due to some critical data that he doesn't trumpet in his talk-show sound bites: These 500,000 or so copying variants are scattered among millions and millions of words in more than five thousand Greek fragments and manuscripts. Embedded within this wealth of witnesses, a half-million copying variants touch only a tiny percentage of the total text.

More importantly, the overwhelming majority of these variants have no impact whatsoever on the meaning of any text. Most of these variations are the result of well-intended attempts to smooth out the grammar or scribal slips that

---

ed. Elijah Hixson and Peter Gurry (Downers Grove: InterVarsity, 2019).

13   Ehrman, *Misquoting Jesus*, 10-11, 69.

14   Peter Gurry, 'The Number of Variants in the Greek New Testament', *New Testament Studies* 62 (2016), 97-121. This estimate does not include spelling variations.

led to divergences in word order, definite articles, and other similar minutiae. Very few of these variants have any impact on the translation of any text; fewer still have any effect on the meaning.

Here's a simple example of the type of variant I'm describing here: In some manuscripts, John 3:3—translated very literally from Greek—begins with these words: 'Answered, the Jesus and said to him'; in other manuscripts of the same verse, the Greek definite article (the word translated 'the') is missing. In many languages—including ancient Greek—the grammar allows a definite article to be placed before proper nouns as well as common nouns. And so, neither one of these sentences is grammatically incorrect. But, since English never places 'the' in front of a name anyway, this difference isn't meaningful or even observable in any English translation. Regardless of the presence or absence of the definite article, the clause comes into English as, 'Jesus answered and said to him' or some simpler wording such as, 'Jesus answered him.' These are the types of copying variants that characterize most of the differences in the New Testament manuscripts.

In the end, only the tiniest fraction of the textual variants has any meaningful impact on the text of the New Testament. Even when textual variants do have some effect, it's almost always possible to discover the earlier reading of the text. For example, at some point in the fourth or fifth centuries A.D., a copyist added this verse to a story in which Jesus healed a physically-challenged man at the Pool of Bethesda:

> They were waiting for the water to move, because an angel from the Lord went down at certain times into the pool and stirred the water; whoever stepped in first after the stirring of the water was healed of any disease. (John 5:4)

The oldest manuscript in which I've seen this extra verse is Codex Alexandrinus, a manuscript that was probably produced in the fifth century A.D. The addition is not present in the third-century codices P66 (Papyrus Bodmer II) or P75 (Papyrus Bodmer XIV—XV), nor does it appear in the fourth-century manuscript known as Codex Sinaiticus.

This addition probably *does* preserve a popular belief about the Pool of Bethesda. Otherwise, the words spoken later by the physically-challenged man wouldn't make sense: 'Sir,' the man pleads with Jesus, 'I have no one to put me into the pool when the water is stirred up; and while I am making my way, someone else steps down ahead of me' (5:7). Perhaps a copyist who knew about this bizarre custom recognized that people's knowledge of the tradition was fading. And so, the copyist added an explanation in the margin of a manuscript that was eventually incorporated into the text. Whatever the reason, textual criticism—the process of analyzing manuscripts to discover the earliest recoverable form of a text—enables biblical scholars to determine which words were added or changed in this text and in the vast majority of other similar cases.

I don't want to give the false impression that every textual dilemma is as straightforward as this additional verse in John's Gospel; many textual differences are far more complex. In some cases, it's difficult to be certain about the initial wording of a text, and the differences do change the meaning. But the crucial question for our purposes is, 'Are these variants so significant that they alter our understanding of Jesus or our interpretation of entire books of the Bible, as *Misquoting Jesus* suggests?'[15]

Let's take a look at three examples from *Misquoting Jesus* to find out.

MARK 1:41: ANGRY JESUS OR COMPASSIONATE JESUS?

Early in Mark's Gospel, the author preserves a story in which Jesus heals a skin-diseased man. The man falls to his knees before Jesus and declares that—if Jesus so chooses—his diseased flesh can be cleansed. According to most of the Greek manuscripts, here's how Jesus responds: 'Moved with pity, Jesus stretched out his hand and touched him' (Mark 1:41). In a few manuscripts, however, there is a variant that results in a very different rendering: 'Becoming angry, Jesus stretched out his hand and touched him.' According

---

15 Ehrman, *Misquoting Jesus*, 132.

to *Misquoting Jesus,* the earlier reading of this text was 'becoming angry', and this variant reshapes the reading of Mark's entire Gospel.

For what it's worth, I think Bart Ehrman is right that the initial text read 'becoming angry' and that a Greek word was changed at some point. But is this textual variant as highly significant as *Misquoting Jesus* seems to suggest? In other words, does this variant actually alter how we understand the entirety of Mark's Gospel?

Not really.

With or without 'becoming angry' in Mark 1:41, Mark's Gospel depicts Jesus as a passionate prophet, rapidly crisscrossing Galilee and Judea as he moves toward his impending encounter with a Roman cross. Jesus becomes vexed and upset when people don't believe him (Mark 3:5; 9:23). And so, how does Jesus respond when the skin-diseased man says, 'If you choose, you can make me clean'? Jesus becomes angry at the disbelief he sees around him (see also Mark 2:6, 24)—but he doesn't respond with hatred or rage. Instead, the righteous anger of Jesus becomes a means that brings about wholeness and healing for the skin-diseased man.

So what happened to this text? It's quite possible that an ancient copyist was uncomfortable with an angry Jesus, so the copyist altered the text to read 'moved with pity' instead of 'becoming angry.' And what if I'm wrong and the earlier reading is 'moved with pity' instead of 'becoming angry'? The Gospel According to Mark makes it clear elsewhere that following Jesus means living with sacrificial compassion for the marginalized, the poor, and the oppressed (Mark 6:34; 8:2; 9:22-23). And so, if Jesus was 'moved with pity' for the skin-diseased man, that would make sense in Mark's Gospel as well. This variant is important, and it's a variant that matters when I teach this text—but it changes nothing about the overall interpretation of Mark's Gospel. Both readings fit perfectly within Mark's overall depiction of Jesus.

JOHN 1:18: ONLY SON OR ONLY GOD?

Something similar can be said about most other variants. In some manuscripts of John 1:18, the author describes Jesus as 'the only Son'. Other manuscripts read 'the only God'. (Some English translations have 'only begotten' or 'one and only' instead of 'only'—but those differences aren't due to any manuscript variant; they're simply different ways of translating the same Greek word.) According to Bart Ehrman, the original reading was 'the only Son', but later copyists changed the text to read 'the only God' to promote their belief that Jesus was divine. However, since early Christian copyists consistently abbreviated both 'Son' and 'God' when they reproduced texts, the difference between these two words would have been only a single letter. It seems equally possible that a careless scribe didn't read his source text clearly and miscopied this verse.

But which wording was in the initial text in the first century A.D.? 'Only Son' or 'only God'?

'The only God' seems to me to fit the structure of this chapter better than 'the only Son'—but, regardless of which option is correct, each wording expresses a truth that's clearly affirmed throughout the rest of the Gospel. In favor of 'only God', the opening verses of John's Gospel already imply that Jesus was uniquely divine (John 1:1-2), and the apostle Thomas unambiguously identifies Jesus as God near the end of the book (John 20:28). In favor of 'only Son', the familiar words of John 3:16 and dozens of other verses throughout John's Gospel refer to Jesus as the Son. Authentic differences do exist in the manuscripts that include the first chapter of John, but—once again—neither of these two possibilities alters the overall claims of this book or of the Bible as a whole.

1 JOHN 5:7-8: AN ADDITION TO A LATIN EDITION THAT ENDED UP IN GREEK

This final example is very different from the others, because virtually everyone agrees on the original wording of the text. In every surviving ancient and medieval Greek manuscript, 1 John 5:7-8 reads something like this when translated into English:

> There are three that testify: the Spirit and the water and the blood, and these three agree.

At some point in the late fourth or early fifth century A.D., the Latin version of this text was expanded to mention the Trinity. The resulting text, rendered in English, reads,

> For there are three that bear witness in heaven: the Father, the Word, and the Holy Spirit; and these three are one. And there are three that bear witness on earth: the Spirit, the water, and the blood; and these three agree as one.

In the early sixteenth century, a scholar named Desiderius Erasmus collated a Greek New Testament to be printed alongside his new Latin translation of the New Testament. Since these extra lines were absent from the Greek manuscripts of 1 John, Erasmus omitted the addition from the first two editions of his Greek New Testament—but this omission upset certain other biblical scholars.

At some point before the publication of the third edition of his Greek New Testament, Erasmus was presented with Codex Montfortianus, a hand-copied edition of the New Testament in Greek. This codex just so happened to include a Greek rendering of the longstanding Latin addition. Some contemporary scholars have speculated that Codex Montfortianus was copied in the early sixteenth century for the purpose of pressuring Erasmus to include the additional text in his Greek New Testament. Regardless of how or why the extra lines ended up in Codex Montfortianus, Erasmus added the text in the third edition of his New Testament.

Every competent scholar in the modern era who has looked at this text has recognized that these lines were added to 1 John centuries after the letter was composed. But Bart Ehrman raises an issue related to this text that would be highly significant if he's correct. According to *Misquoting Jesus*, this text is 'the only passage in the entire Bible that explicitly delineates the doctrine of the Trinity.'[16] 'Trinity', of course, describes the essential Christian belief that God is one God in three persons—God the Holy Spirit, God the Son, and God the Father. Without this verse, Bart Ehrman claims, the Bible never clearly teaches the doctrine of the Trinity.

But does the Trinity really hang so heavily on this single verse?

Not even close.

In fact, the Gospel According to Matthew delineates the Trinity no less clearly than this clause that an overly-creative copyist added to the Latin text of 1 John. According to Matthew 28:19, God is one God ('in the name', singular) in three persons ('of the Father and of the Son and of the Holy Spirit'). The reference to the Trinity was added to

---

16   Ehrman, *Misquoting* Jesus, 81.

1 John 5 *after* the Apostles' Creed and the Creed of Nicaea were already universally embraced in the churches. Both of these creeds are explicitly Trinitarian confessions of faith. If the sole biblical text that clearly delineates the Trinity didn't even exist until the late fourth or early fifth century, from where did Christians in the early fourth century derive their dogged commitment to the Trinity as an essential component of Christian faith?

In fact, the doctrine of the Trinity was firmly established on the basis of the New Testament long before anyone made any additions to John's first letter. This commitment grew from Matthew 28:19 and a number of other texts in which the authors of the New Testament articulated their emerging recognition that God is one God in three persons (see, for examples, John 14:16-17; 2 Cor. 13:14). No, this text in 1 John didn't exist in the earliest manuscripts—but this is far from the only verse to delineate the doctrine of the Trinity, and it's not even close to constituting a theologically-significant alteration of the text.

ARE THE CHANGES SIGNIFICANT OR NOT?

Throughout *Misquoting Jesus,* Bart Ehrman rightly points out that there are hundreds of thousands of copying variants, and these variants produce complex questions about a handful of biblical texts. And yet, none of these variants changes any vital belief that Christians hold about God, about Jesus, or about God's work in the world. Regardless of whether the Bible is true or false, no Christian doctrine or practice is diminished, decided, or determined by any textually uncertain passage of Scripture.

From time to time, Bart Ehrman does manage to dampen his critiques with candid concessions that sound strangely similar to what I've argued in this chapter. For example, Ehrman acknowledges at one point in *Misquoting Jesus*: 'I continue to think that even if we cannot be 100 percent certain about what we can attain to, … it is at least possible to get back to the *oldest* and *earliest* stage of the manuscript tradition for each of the books of the New Testament.'[17] Elsewhere, he admits that,

> it is probably safe to say that the copying of early Christian texts was by and large a 'conservative' process. The scribes … were intent on 'conserving' the textual tradition they were passing on. Their ultimate concern was not to modify the tradition, but to preserve it for themselves and for those who would follow them. Most scribes, no doubt, tried to do a faithful job in making sure that the text they reproduced was the same text they inherited.[18]

In his earlier book *Lost Christianities,* Ehrman states that it is possible to 'reconstruct the oldest form of the words of the

---

17   Ehrman, *Misquoting Jesus*, 62.

18   Ehrman, *Misquoting Jesus*, 177.

New Testament with reasonable (though not 100 percent) accuracy.'[19]

And yet, it seems that Ehrman wants 'to have his text-critical cake and eat it, too.'[20] Only a few pages after affirming that it is possible to recover the earliest stage of the manuscript tradition, Ehrman refers to Christianity as 'a textually oriented religion whose texts have been changed' in 'lots of significant' ways.[21] But why are the changes scattered among thousands of manuscripts so significant if it is possible to recover—by Ehrman's own admission—'the oldest form of the words'? The only answer I can give is that, in the end, these changes really aren't that significant after all. Despite the many differences among the manuscripts, the process of transmission has resulted in a remarkably reliable and well-preserved Bible.

DIFFERENT TEXTS, SAME TRUTH

This morning, I gathered in the library archives with a group of my doctoral students to teach them about the history of the Greek New Testament. Class is over now, the students are gone, and there are four books left on the table. The oldest of the four volumes is GA2358, an

---

19 Ehrman, *Lost Christianities*, 221.

20 Michael J. Kruger, 'Review of *Misquoting Jesus: The Story Behind Who Changed the Bible and Why* (Bart Ehrman)', in *Journal of the Evangelical Theological Society* 49 (June 2006), 389.

21 Ehrman, *Misquoting Jesus*, 69.

eleventh-century manuscript of the Gospels also known as Codex Robertsonianus. Two of the volumes were published in the sixteenth century: one of them is the third edition of Erasmus's Greek New Testament; the other is a far smaller Greek text printed in Geneva in 1552 for John Calvin's students. The last and latest text is my Tyndale House Greek New Testament, published only a few years ago.

Not one of the Greek texts of the Gospels on this table agrees in every detail with all of the others. There are, in fact, thousands of differences that distinguish these four volumes from one another. Three of the four texts include the extra verse in John 5 about the Pool of Bethesda. One of these texts reads 'only God' in John 1:18, while the others have 'only Son'. And yet, let's suppose that I selected one of these volumes to be my exclusive copy of the Gospels and that I never had access to the text in any of the others. *No matter which of the four texts I chose, no textual variant in any of these books would change anything that I believe.* Not one of the thousands of variants represented on this table threatens any aspect of my faith in the resurrected Jesus. The text of the Bible has not been preserved perfectly—but it has been preserved sufficiently to sustain every vital truth that Christians confess.

MISSING TEXTS ACCORDING TO *MISQUOTING JESUS*

The paperback edition of *Misquoting Jesus* includes a section that claims to present significant texts that are missing from some biblical manuscripts. It is true that these texts are absent in many biblical manuscripts, but these absences are far less significant than *Misquoting Jesus* seems to suggest.

What's missing?	*Why is this significant, according to* Misquoting Jesus?	*Is this variant so significant that it changes any Christian belief or practice?*
John 7:53– 8:11	'Many scholars think that [John 7:53—8:11] was probably a well-known story, circulating in the oral tradition about Jesus, which at some point was added in the margin of a manuscript. From there, some scribe or another thought that the marginal note was meant to be part of the text.'	No vital beliefs about Jesus or about Scripture appear in this text. If the story was part of an early oral tradition, it is possible that the event authentically occurred, even if it didn't appear in the earliest manuscripts of John's Gospel. This section was not part of the initial form of John's Gospel.

Luke 24:12, 51	'It supports so well the ... position that Jesus ... had a real, physical body. ... It stresses the physicality of Jesus's departure. ... It may be that a scribe involved in these controversies modified his text in order to stress the point.'	No, the physicality of Jesus's resurrection is already stressed elsewhere in Luke's Gospel. Jesus broke bread and ate fish after his resurrection (Luke 24:30, 42), both of which are clearly physical actions that required the resurrection of a physical body.
Luke 22:43-44	'Rather than entering his passion with fear and trembling, in anguish over his coming fate, the Jesus of Luke goes to his death calm and in control. ... It is clear that Luke does not share Mark's understanding that Jesus was in anguish, bordering on despair.'	No. Simply because Luke emphasized one aspect of Jesus's death—the willing submission of a righteous man to the cross—doesn't mean that his understanding of the death of Jesus contradicted Mark's perspective. It simply means that Luke emphasized an aspect that Mark did not.

Luke 22:20	'Luke ... has a different understanding of the way in which Jesus' death leads to salvation than does Mark (and Paul, and other early Christian writers). ... Jesus' death is ... *extremely* important for Luke—but not as an atonement. Instead, Jesus' death is what makes people realize their guilt before God.'	No. In the first place, this text also appears in the writings of Paul, with whom Luke was associated (1 Cor. 11:23-25). Even if the text was not part of the initial edition of Luke's Gospel, Luke's focus on the death of Jesus as a means for revealing humanity's guilt does not imply that he didn't understand Jesus's death as an atonement as well. Different emphases do not amount to contradictory understandings of the same event.

Mark 16:9-20	'Scribes thought the ending [of Mark's Gospel] was too abrupt. ... To resolve the problem, scribes added an ending [Mark 16:9-20].'	No. It's true that the original version of the Gospel According to Mark may have ended at Mark 16:8. However, the physical resurrection of Jesus and his subsequent appearances to his disciples are still implied throughout Mark's Gospel (see 9:9; 14:28). The references to new tongues, snakes, and poison—whatever their meaning may be—appear in other biblical texts too (Ps. 69:21, 29; Isaiah 11:8; Luke 10:19; Acts 2:4).

RECOMMENDED READING

Blomberg, Craig. *The Historical Reliability of the New Testament.* (Nashville: B&H, 2016).

Hixson, Elijah, and Peter Gurry (eds). *Myths and Mistakes in New Testament Textual Criticism.* (Downers Grove: InterVarsity, 2019).

Perrin, Nicholas. *Lost in Transmission?* (Nashville: Nelson, 2008).

Stewart, Robert (ed.). *The Reliability of the New Testament.* (Philadelphia: Fortress, 2011).

Wallace, Daniel (ed.). *Revisiting the Corruption of the New Testament.* (Grand Rapids: Kregel, 2011).

Also available in the *Big Ten* Series…

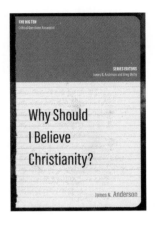

Why Should I Believe Christianity?

James N. Anderson

Some people boldly claim, 'Christianity is fine for some, but it isn't for me'. Others feel it is just outdated and irrelevant. For better or worse, everyone in the Western world has come into contact with Christianity: we all have some opinion on it.

James N. Anderson, with a clear, humorous logic, explores what Christianity really claims, and shows the underlying reason and consistency behind these claims. By the end of *Why Should I Believe Christianity?*, while you may not agree with the Christian worldview, it is impossible to be left sitting on the fence.

ISBN 978-1-7819-1869-2

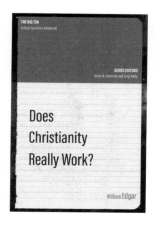

Does Christianity Really Work?

WILLIAM EDGAR

Wasn't the South African Apartheid supported by Christians? Weren't the Crusades motivated by greed, but advocated by the church? Don't phoney television preachers manipulate viewers into donating money? William Edgar addresses these and other questions honestly, without attempting to dismiss or explain away their uncomfortable realities. He displays the good aspects of the church even more brilliantly through frankly and Biblically acknowledging the bad. If you have ever asked the question *Does Christianity Really Work?* this will be an interesting and enlightening read, whatever your prior convictions.

ISBN 978-1-7819-1775-6

Why Is There Evil in the World (and So Much of It?)

GREG WELTY

Many people argue that the presence of evil in the world is proof that God cannot exist, or if He does exist, cannot be good or all-powerful.

Greg Welty uses biblical exegesis alongside his experience as a philosopher to present a different conclusion. God, the sovereign Creator and Sustainer of the world, really does work all things for good. A must-read for anyone struggling with this issue.

ISBN 978-1-5271-0141-8

How Could a Loving God Send Anyone to Hell?

Benjamin M. Skaug

The question of whether God can be loving and also send people to hell is one people have been asking for a long time. Surely a God who sends people to hell cannot love them? Starting with a look at who God is and how we relate to Him, Benjamin Skaug looks at what the Bible has to say about the difficult topic of hell.

ISBN 978-1-5271-0473-0

Christian Focus Publications

Our mission statement –

STAYING FAITHFUL
In dependence upon God we seek to impact the world
through literature faithful to His infallible Word, the Bible.
Our aim is to ensure that the Lord Jesus Christ is presented
as the only hope to obtain forgiveness of sin, live a useful life
and look forward to heaven with Him.

Our books are published in four imprints:

CHRISTIAN
FOCUS

Popular works including biographies, commentaries, basic
doctrine and Christian living.

CHRISTIAN
HERITAGE

Books representing some of the
best material from the rich heritage of the church.

MENTOR

Books written at a level suitable
for Bible College and seminary
students, pastors, and other serious readers. The imprint includes
commentaries, doctrinal studies,
examination of current issues and
church history.

CF4•K

Children's books for quality Bible
teaching and for all age groups:
Sunday school curriculum, puzzle
and activity books; personal and family devotional titles, biographies and
inspirational stories – because you
are never too young to know Jesus!

Christian Focus Publications Ltd,
Geanies House, Fearn, Ross-shire,
IV20 1TW, Scotland, United Kingdom.
www.christianfocus.com